Praise for *HIS Story*

HIS Story is a simple masterpiece in the truest sense of the word. It is simply the four gospels woven together into a single chronological narrative. It is like getting Matthew, Mark, Luke, and John in a men's quartet to sing a single harmonized song. As you read *HIS Story*, the richness of all four narratives flow together to form a rich and comprehensive tapestry of the life of Jesus. The sub-title is true: "Get to Know Jesus like you've never known him before." **–Dr. Mark Moore, author of *The Chronological Life of Christ***

Chandler Christian Church has found a way to harmonize the four Gospels into a seamless story in *HIS Story*. It is God's Word in a simple to understand form and format. What could be better than reading and learning about the life of Christ? – **Dave Stone, Senior Pastor of Southeast Christian Church, Louisville, KY**

This was something that just pulled me and my kids deeper in our faith and relationship with God. I was amazed at how deeply my kids (ages 7 & 4) seemed to understand and absorb. We weren't just impacted; we were changed. Honestly, I'd really like to do it again, now. **–Reader**

Our son is ten years old, and reading *HIS Story* has been the first time that he has had the chance to read and understand the story of Jesus in its full power. **–Reader**

I've always believed that Jesus was the Son of God, but before, He was THE central character of the Bible. Now He's my friend . . . He holds my hand during difficult times and comforts me with a gentle arm around my shoulder. **–Reader**

HIS Story has had such a positive impact on me. It has really broken down the stories in such a basic way that I can understand/comprehend and then feel confident to witness to others. In addition, I have been part of a small group and we have been speaking about "His Story." It is refreshing that other folks learned as much, if not more, about Jesus and His life on Earth. **–Reader**

The chronology or putting all four gospel books into chronological order helped understand how His Story is One Story. Being able to understand how the story fits together helped me increase head knowledge and my faith in the validity and truth of all the books. **–Reader**

We thought it was refreshing and challenging to go thru the basics and simplicity of the Christian life and Jesus' love for us. He is faithful and He is our precious Savior. His grace is brought home again to me and heals the holes in my soul again and again. **–Reader**

I have grown closer to God and encouraged my family to come to church. *HIS Story* has touched the life of my brother who has not been to church in 15+ years. He has recently surrendered his life to Christ. *HIS Story* has also re-established my relationship with Christ. Praise God! **–Reader**

HIS Story has had a huge impact on our entire family's lives. It has changed the nature of the discussions we have and the decisions we make as a family. *HIS Story* and the discussions it has inspired played a huge role in helping our son embrace Jesus. **–Reader**

Know Jesus Like Never Before.

NLT.

HIS Story

Published by HIS Story
Chandler, AZ 85286
www.knowHISstory.com

ISBN 978-0-9854516-0-8

Produced with the assistance of Chandler Christian Church. The concept was original with Roger Storms, edited and compiled by Matt Myers, and chapter contributions were made by Matt Myers, Roger Storms, Don Anderson, and Austin Martin.

Cover Design and Maps: Real Life Ministries, Jeremie Lederman
Illustrations: Janet Stratman
Daily Questions: Real Life Ministries

Proofreading by Peachtree Editorial Service, Peachtree City, GA

Printed in the United States of America

Contents

~ Timeline

DATE*	CH.	EVENT

His Preparation Years

5 B.C.	1	Jesus is born
1 A.D.		
5 A.D.	1	Jesus in the Temple at age 12
10 A.D.		

His 1st Year of Ministry

26 A.D.	2	Baptized by John
	2	Jesus' ministry begins
	2	First miracle: Water to wine at Cana
27 A.D.	2	First Passover, Jesus cleanses the Temple
	2	Interview with Nicodemus, John 3:16
	2	Interview with the woman at the well in Samaria
	3	Calls His first disciples
	3	First ministry tour through Galilee

His 2nd Year of Ministry

28 A.D.	4	Second Passover
	4	Heals lame man at the pool on Sabbath
	4	Twelve disciples are appointed
	4	Jesus preaches the Sermon on the Mount
	5	Second ministry tour through Galilee
	6	Third ministry tour through Galilee— Sends out disciples two by two
	6	Death of Jesus' cousin, John the Baptist
29 A.D.	6	Third Passover
	6	Feeding of 5,000
	6	Jesus walks on water

Timeline

DATE*	CH.	EVENT
His 3rd Year of Ministry		
29 A.D.	7	Feeding of the 4,000
	7	Peter's great confession
	7	Jesus predicts His death for the first time
	7	The Transfiguration
	8	Jesus sends out 72 on mission
30 A.D.	9	Jesus eats at Zacchaeus' home
His Final Week		
Final Week	10	Sunday: Triumphal Entry into Jerusalem
	10	Monday: Jesus cleanses the Temple a second time and curses a fig tree
	10	Tuesday: Jesus rebukes the Pharisees and privately predicts Jerusalem's fall and His second coming
	11	Thursday: Fourth Passover
	11	Last Supper with the twelve disciples
	11	Jesus washes the feet of His disciples
	12	Jesus prays in the garden of Gethsemane
	12	Jesus' arrest and trials
	12	Friday: Jesus is crucified and buried
	13	Sunday: Resurrection
	14	Jesus' Great Commission and Ascension

*Dates are approximate

Welcome to HIS Story:
Know Jesus Like Never Before

Daily Bible reading is an important part of spiritual growth and maturity. This chronological harmony of the life of Jesus was adapted to create a tool to assist you, the reader, in your pursuit of spiritual growth and maturity. We wanted to make the harmony read smoothly and easily, so that you can read it just like you would read a novel. But, because HIS Story is not an ordinary story, we wanted to provide you the opportunity to interact with it in a different way; to read *and* reflect – allowing His story to move from your head to your heart!

- **READ** HIS Story daily, one chapter a week. Carve out a regular time and space in your world each day for this special appointment with God.

- *REFLECT* on what you are reading – moving it from your head to your heart. Each chapter is broken into smaller daily readings, as noted by the "Reflection" questions. Taking time to reflect on God's word, to linger and soak it up, like a good marinade, greatly enhances and changes the flavor of your experience. Don't just read this book, interact with it. Underline it. Write your own thoughts in the margins. Make it *your* book, personalize it.

⌒ Denotes the end of that day's reading.

🖑 Denotes the head level question that helps you make observations of the text – engaging the text at a head level.

♥ Denotes the heart/hands level question that helps you to interact with the text at a heart and hands level; moving from information to inspiration and hopefully perspiration – putting into action in your life.

God designed us to be in relationship with Him and with others. So if you've come this far, maybe you'd be willing to go a little farther. Is there someone you can share your journey with – someone with whom you can share and discuss what you're reading – helping to move it from your heart to your hands in ways that impact how you live, love and serve?

We pray that HIS Story will change the way you live and view life, which will lead to an absolute conviction that this man Jesus is exactly who He claimed to be – the one and only Son of God!

His Preparation Years

Travels in His Preparation Years

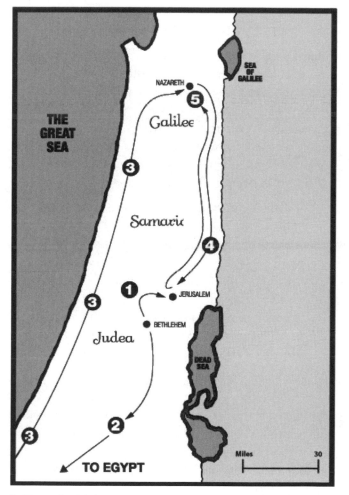

1. From Bethlehem to Jerusalem and return.

2. From Bethlehem to Egypt.

3. From Egypt to Nazareth.

4. From Nazareth to Jerusalem.

5. From Jerusalem to Nazareth.

Chapter 1

The Birth of Hope

Many people have set out to write accounts about the events that have been fulfilled among us. They used the eyewitness reports circulating among us from the early disciples. Having carefully investigated everything from the beginning, I also have decided to write a careful account for you, most honorable Theophilus,[1] so you can be certain of the truth of everything you were taught.

In the beginning the Word already existed. The Word was with God, and the Word was God. He existed in the beginning with God. God created everything through him, and nothing was created except through him. The Word gave life to everything that was created, and his life brought light to everyone. The light shines in the darkness, and the darkness can never extinguish it.

God sent a man, John the Baptist, to tell about the light so that everyone might believe because of his testimony. John himself was not the light; he was simply a witness to tell about the light. The one who is the true light, who gives light to everyone, was coming into the world.

He came into the very world he created, but the world didn't recognize him. He came to his own

---

[1] **Theophilus:** Literally means "friend of God." He was the recipient of Luke's Gospel as well as Luke's second book, Acts. Luke wanted to give an orderly account to him so that he might know for certain the things that he was being taught.

people, and even they rejected him. But to all who believed him and accepted him, he gave the right to become children of God. They are reborn—not with a physical birth resulting from human passion or plan, but a birth that comes from God.

So the Word became human and made his home among us. He was full of unfailing love and faithfulness. And we have seen his glory, the glory of the Father's one and only Son.

John testified about him when he shouted to the crowds, "This is the one I was talking about when I said, 'Someone is coming after me who is far greater than I am, for he existed long before me.' "

From his abundance we have all received one gracious blessing after another. For the law was given through Moses, but God's unfailing love and faithful-ness came through Jesus Christ. No one has ever seen God. But the unique One, who is himself God, is near to the Father's heart. He has revealed God to us.

Introducing Jesus is no small task. Two of the Gospel writers, Matthew and Luke, provide us with Jesus' family tree, which is called a genealogy. It may not sound exciting, but a genealogy in Jesus' day served the same purpose that a resume does today. So what will Jesus' resume tell us?

This is a record of the ancestors of Jesus the Messiah, a descendant of King David[2] and of Abraham.

---

[2] **David**: Anointed to replace Saul as Israel's king. David's success was unprecedented. God promised David that his throne would last for eternity. Jesus fulfills this promise.

Genealogy of Jesus According to Matthew

Matthew's main agenda, through his genealogy, is to show how Jesus is the King of the Jews. He begins with Abraham and moves forward towards Jesus. Surprisingly, Matthew includes a few seedy characters that most would have omitted, since Jewish genealogies weren't required to be complete. But it's important for him to show what kind of King Jesus will be—a King of grace.

Abraham was the father of Isaac.

Isaac was the father of Jacob.

Jacob was the father of Judah and his brothers.

Judah was the father of Perez and Zerah
(whose mother was Tamar).

Perez was the father of Hezron.

Hezron was the father of Ram.

Ram was the father of Amminadab.

Amminadab was the father of Nahshon.

Nahshon was the father of Salmon.

Salmon was the father of Boaz (whose mother was Rahab).

Boaz was the father of Obed (whose mother was Ruth).

Obed was the father of Jesse.

Jesse was the father of King David.

David was the father of Solomon
(whose mother was Bathsheba, the widow of Uriah).

Solomon was the father of Rehoboam.

Rehoboam was the father of Abijah.

Abijah was the father of Asa.

Asa was the father of Jehoshaphat.

Jehoshaphat was the father of Jehoram.

Jehoram was the father of Uzziah.
Uzziah was the father of Jotham.
Jotham was the father of Ahaz.
Ahaz was the father of Hezekiah.
Hezekiah was the father of Manasseh.
Manasseh was the father of Amon.
Amon was the father of Josiah.
Josiah was the father of Jehoiachin and his brothers
(born at the time of the exile to Babylon).
After the Babylonian exile:
Jehoiachin was the father of Shealtiel.
Shealtiel was the father of Zerubbabel.
Zerubbabel was the father of Abiud.
Abiud was the father of Eliakim.
Eliakim was the father of Azor.
Azor was the father of Zadok.
Zadok was the father of Akim.
Akim was the father of Eliud.
Eliud was the father of Eleazar.
Eleazar was the father of Matthan.
Matthan was the father of Jacob.
Jacob was the father of Joseph, the husband of Mary.
Mary gave birth to Jesus, who is called the Messiah.

All those listed above include fourteen generations from
Abraham to David, fourteen from David to the
Babylonian exile, and fourteen from the Babylonian exile
to the Messiah.

Genealogy of Jesus According to Luke

Luke's genealogy begins with Jesus and then moves backward to the very first man, Adam. Both genealogies tell us that God loves us and names us; God can use unknown and fallen people to accomplish His good purpose.

Jesus was known as the son of Joseph.
Joseph was the son of Heli.
Heli was the son of Matthat.
Matthat was the son of Levi.
Levi was the son of Melki.
Melki was the son of Jannai.
Jannai was the son of Joseph.
Joseph was the son of Mattathias.
Mattathias was the son of Amos.
Amos was the son of Nahum.
Nahum was the son of Esli.
Esli was the son of Naggai.
Naggai was the son of Maath.
Maath was the son of Mattathias.
Mattathias was the son of Semein.
Semein was the son of Josech.
Josech was the son of Joda.
Joda was the son of Joanan.
Joanan was the son of Rhesa.
Rhesa was the son of Zerubbabel.
Zerubbabel was the son of Shealtiel.
Shealtiel was the son of Neri.
Neri was the son of Melki.
Melki was the son of Addi.
Addi was the son of Cosam.
Cosam was the son of Elmadam.
Elmadam was the son of Er.
Er was the son of Joshua.
Joshua was the son of Eliezer.
Eliezer was the son of Jorim.
Jorim was the son of Matthat.
Matthat was the son of Levi.
Levi was the son of Simeon.
Simeon was the son of Judah.
Judah was the son of Joseph.

Joseph was the son of Jonam.
Jonam was the son of Eliakim.
Eliakim was the son of Melea.
Melea was the son of Menna.
Menna was the son of Mattatha.
Mattatha was the son of Nathan.
Nathan was the son of David.
David was the son of Jesse.
Jesse was the son of Obed.
Obed was the son of Boaz.
Boaz was the son of Salmon.
Salmon was the son of Nahshon.
Nahshon was the son of Amminadab.
Amminadab was the son of Admin.
Admin was the son of Arni.
Arni was the son of Hezron.
Hezron was the son of Perez.
Perez was the son of Judah.
Judah was the son of Jacob.
Jacob was the son of Isaac.
Isaac was the son of Abraham.
Abraham was the son of Terah.
Terah was the son of Nahor.
Nahor was the son of Serug.
Serug was the son of Reu.
Reu was the son of Peleg.
Peleg was the son of Eber.
Eber was the son of Shelah.
Shelah was the son of Cainan.
Cainan was the son of Arphaxad.
Arphaxad was the son of Shem.
Shem was the son of Noah.
Noah was the son of Lamech.
Lamech was the son of Methuselah.
Methuselah was the son of Enoch.
Enoch was the son of Jared.
Jared was the son of Mahalalel.
Mahalalel was the son of Kenan.
Kenan was the son of Enosh.
Enosh was the son of Seth.
Seth was the son of Adam.
Adam was the son of God.

Reflection

From to-
day's reading,
what do you
think the writ-
ers want us to
know about
who Jesus is?

How has
today's reading
given you new
insights in how
you could
introduce Jesus
to someone?

The Gospels begin by showing the big picture of the person and purpose of Christ. It seems strange to just now be getting to Jesus' birth. This next section weaves back and forth between the birth stories of two cousins—Jesus and John. Birth narratives like these are common in ancient biographies of famous people. They answer the question: How do we account for a life such as this?

When Herod[3] was king of Judea, there was a Jewish priest named Zechariah. He was a member of the priestly order of Abijah, and his wife, Elizabeth, was also from the priestly line of Aaron. Zechariah and Elizabeth were righteous in God's eyes, careful to obey all of the Lord's commandments and regulations. They had no children because Elizabeth was unable to conceive, and they were both very old.

One day Zechariah was serving God in the Temple, for his order was on duty that week. As was the custom of the priests, he was chosen by lot to enter the sanctuary of the Lord and burn incense. While the incense was being burned, a great crowd stood outside, praying.

While Zechariah was in the sanctuary, an angel of the Lord appeared to him, standing to the right of the incense altar. Zechariah was shaken and overwhelmed with fear when he saw him. But the

---

[3] **Herod**: Historians customarily introduced a narrative by listing the names of reigning kings or governors, which provided the approximate time of the narrative. Herod the Great was officially king of Judea from 37 to 4 B.C. This is not the same Herod who had John the Baptist killed later.

angel said, "Don't be afraid, Zechariah! God has heard your prayer. Your wife, Elizabeth, will give you a son, and you are to name him John. You will have great joy and gladness, and many will rejoice at his birth, for he will be great in the eyes of the Lord. He must never touch wine or other alcoholic drinks. He will be filled with the Holy Spirit, even before his birth. And he will turn many Israelites to the Lord their God. He will be a man with the spirit and power of Elijah. He will prepare the people for the coming of the Lord. He will turn the hearts of the fathers to their children, and he will cause those who are rebellious to accept the wisdom of the godly."

Zechariah said to the angel, "How can I be sure this will happen? I'm an old man now, and my wife is also well along in years."

Then the angel said, "I am Gabriel! I stand in the very presence of God. It was he who sent me to bring you this good news! But now, since you didn't believe what I said, you will be silent and unable to speak until the child is born. For my words will certainly be fulfilled at the proper time."

Meanwhile, the people were waiting for Zechariah to come out of the sanctuary, wondering why he was taking so long. When he finally did come out, he couldn't speak to them. Then they realized from his gestures and his silence that he must have seen a vision in the sanctuary.

When Zechariah's week of service in the Temple was over, he returned home. Soon afterward his wife, Elizabeth, became pregnant and went into seclusion for five months. "How kind the Lord is!" she exclaimed. "He has taken away my disgrace of having no children."

In the sixth month of Elizabeth's pregnancy, God sent the angel Gabriel to Nazareth, a village in Galilee, to a virgin named Mary. She was engaged to be married to a man named Joseph, a descendant of King David. Gabriel appeared to her and said, "Greetings, favored woman! The Lord is with you!"

Confused and disturbed, Mary tried to think what the angel could mean. "Don't be afraid, Mary," the angel told her, "for you have found favor with God! You will conceive and give birth to a son, and you will name him Jesus. He will be very great and will be called the Son of the Most High. The Lord God will give him the throne of his ancestor David. And he will reign over Israel forever; his Kingdom will never end!"

Mary asked the angel, "But how can this happen? I am a virgin."

The angel replied, "The Holy Spirit will come upon you, and the power of the Most High will overshadow you. So the baby to be born will be holy, and he will be called the Son of God. What's more, your relative Elizabeth has become pregnant in her old age! People used to say she was barren, but she's now in her sixth month. For nothing is impossible with God."

Mary responded, "I am the Lord's servant. May everything you have said about me come true." And then the angel left her.

A few days later Mary hurried to the hill country of Judea, to the town where Zechariah lived. She entered the house and greeted Elizabeth. At the sound of Mary's greeting, Elizabeth's child leaped within her, and Elizabeth was filled with the Holy Spirit.

Elizabeth gave a glad cry and exclaimed to Mary, "God has blessed you above all women, and your child is blessed. Why am I so honored, that the mother of my Lord should visit me? When I heard your greeting, the baby in my womb jumped for joy. You are blessed because you believed that the Lord would do what he said."

Mary responded,

"Oh, how my soul praises the Lord. How my spirit rejoices in God my Savior! For he took notice of his lowly servant girl, and from now on all generations will call me blessed. For the Mighty One is holy, and he has done great things for me. He shows mercy from generation to generation to all who fear him. His mighty arm has done tremendous things! He has scattered the proud and haughty ones. He has brought down princes from their thrones and exalted the humble. He has filled the hungry with good things and sent the rich away with empty hands. He has helped his servant Israel and remembered to be merciful. For he made this promise to our ancestors, to Abraham and his children forever."

Mary stayed with Elizabeth about three months and then went back to her own home.

When it was time for Elizabeth's baby to be born, she gave birth to a son. And when her neighbors and relatives heard that the Lord had been very merciful to her, everyone rejoiced with her.

When the baby was eight days old, they all came for the circumcision[4] ceremony. They wanted to name him Zechariah, after his father. But Elizabeth said, "No! His name is John!"

"What?" they exclaimed. "There is no one in all your family by that name." So they used gestures to ask the baby's father what he wanted to name him. He motioned for a writing tablet, and to everyone's surprise he wrote, "His name is John." Instantly Zechariah could speak again, and he began praising God.

Awe fell upon the whole neighborhood, and the news of what had happened spread throughout the Judean hills. Everyone who heard about it reflected on these events and asked, "What will this child turn out to be?" For the hand of the Lord was surely upon him in a special way.

Then his father, Zechariah, was filled with the Holy Spirit and gave this prophecy:

> "Praise the Lord, the God of Israel, because he has visited and redeemed his people. He has sent us a mighty Savior from the royal line of his servant David, just as he promised through his holy prophets long ago. Now we will be saved from our enemies and from all who hate us. He has been merciful to our ancestors by remembering his sacred covenant—the covenant he swore with an oath to our ancestor Abraham. We have been rescued

---

[4] **circumcision**: A surgical removal of the foreskin of the male, performed on the eighth day following birth. In the Old Testament this ritual symbolized the baby's entrance into the Hebrew community.

from our enemies so we can serve God without fear, in holiness and righteousness for as long as we live.

"And you, my little son, will be called the prophet of the Most High, because you will prepare the way for the Lord. You will tell his people how to find salvation through forgiveness of their sins. Because of God's tender mercy, the morning light from heaven is about to break upon us, to give light to those who sit in darkness and in the shadow of death, and to guide us to the path of peace."

John grew up and became strong in spirit. And he lived in the wilderness until he began his public ministry to Israel.

What is similar and different between Zechariah's, Elizabeth's and Mary's experiences?

How do you respond when you sense God is calling you to step out in faith?

This is how Jesus the Messiah was born. His mother, Mary, was engaged to be married to Joseph. But before the marriage took place, while she was still a virgin, she became pregnant through the power of the Holy Spirit. Joseph, her fiancé, was a good man and did not want to disgrace her publicly, so he decided to break the engagement quietly.

As he considered this, an angel of the Lord appeared to him in a dream. "Joseph, son of David," the angel said, "do not be afraid to take Mary as your wife. For the child within her was conceived by the Holy Spirit. And she will have a son, and you are to name him Jesus, for he will save his people from their sins."

All of this occurred to fulfill the Lord's message through his prophet:

"Look! The virgin will conceive a child! She will give birth to a son, and they will call him Immanuel, which means 'God is with us.' "

When Joseph woke up, he did as the angel of the Lord commanded and took Mary as his wife. But he did not have sexual relations with her until her son was born. And Joseph named him Jesus.

At that time the Roman emperor, Augustus, decreed that a census should be taken throughout the Roman Empire. (This was the first census taken when Quirinius was governor of Syria.) All returned to their own ancestral towns to register for this census. And because Joseph was a descendant of King David, he had to go to Bethlehem in Judea, David's ancient home. He traveled there from the village of Nazareth in Galilee. He took with him Mary, his fiancée, who was now obviously pregnant.

And while they were there, the time came for her baby to be born. She gave birth to her first child, a son. She wrapped him snugly in strips of cloth and laid him in a manger, because there was no lodging available for them.

That night there were shepherds staying in the fields nearby, guarding their flocks of sheep. Suddenly, an angel of the Lord appeared among them, and the radiance of the Lord's glory surrounded them. They were terrified, but the angel reassured them. "Don't be afraid!" he said. "I bring you good news that will bring great joy to all people. The Savior—yes, the Messiah, the Lord—has been born today in Bethlehem, the city of David! And you will recognize him by this sign: You will find a baby wrapped snugly in strips of cloth, lying in a manger."

Suddenly, the angel was joined by a vast host of others—the armies of heaven—praising God and saying,

> "Glory to God in highest heaven, and peace on earth to those with whom God is pleased."

When the angels had returned to heaven, the shepherds said to each other, "Let's go to Bethlehem! Let's see this thing that has happened, which the Lord has told us about."

They hurried to the village and found Mary and Joseph. And there was the baby, lying in the manger. After seeing him, the shepherds told everyone what had happened and what the angel had said to them about this child. All who heard the shepherds' story were astonished, but Mary kept all these things in her heart and thought about them often. The shepherds went back to their flocks, glorifying and praising God for all they had heard and seen. It was just as the angel had told them.

Eight days later, when the baby was circumcised, he was named Jesus, the name given him by the angel even before he was conceived.

⚜

Then it was time for their purification offering, as required by the law of Moses after the birth of a child; so his parents took him to Jerusalem to present him to the Lord. The law of the Lord says, "If a woman's first child is a boy, he must be dedicated to the LORD." So they offered the sacrifice

Reflection

How does Joseph respond to what is happening in his life?

When the shepherds told their story people were astonished. When has someone's story moved you to be in awe of God? With whom can you share what God has done in your life?

required in the law of the Lord— "either a pair of turtledoves or two young pigeons."

At that time there was a man in Jerusalem named Simeon. He was righteous and devout and was eagerly waiting for the Messiah to come and rescue Israel. The Holy Spirit was upon him and had revealed to him that he would not die until he had seen the Lord's Messiah. That day the Spirit led him to the Temple. So when Mary and Joseph came to present the baby Jesus to the Lord as the law required, Simeon was there. He took the child in his arms and praised God, saying,

> "Sovereign Lord, now let your servant die in peace, as you have promised. I have seen your salvation, which you have prepared for all people. He is a light to reveal God to the nations, and he is the glory of your people Israel!"

Jesus' parents were amazed at what was being said about him. Then Simeon blessed them, and he said to Mary, the baby's mother, "This child is destined to cause many in Israel to fall, but he will be a joy to many others. He has been sent as a sign from God, but many will oppose him. As a result, the deepest thoughts of many hearts will be revealed. And a sword will pierce your very soul."

Anna, a prophet, was also there in the Temple. She was the daughter of Phanuel from the tribe of Asher, and she was very old. Her husband died whenthey had been married only seven years. Then she lived as a widow to the age of eighty-four. She never left the Temple but stayed there day and night, worshiping God with fasting and prayer. She came along just as Simeon was talking with Mary and

Joseph, and she began praising God. She talked about the child to everyone who had been waiting expectantly for God to rescue Jerusalem.

⟡

Jesus was born in Bethlehem in Judea, during the reign of King Herod. About that time some wise men from eastern lands arrived in Jerusalem, asking, "Where is the newborn king of the Jews? We saw his star as it rose, and we have come to worship him."

King Herod was deeply disturbed when he heard this, as was everyone in Jerusalem. He called a meeting of the leading priests and teachers of religious law and asked, "Where is the Messiah supposed to be born?"

"In Bethlehem in Judea," they said, "for this is what the prophet wrote:

'And you, O Bethlehem in the land of Judah, are not least among the ruling cities of Judah, for a ruler will come from you who will be the shepherd for my people Israel.' "

Then Herod called for a private meeting with the wise men, and he learned from them the time when the star first appeared. Then he told them, "Go to Bethlehem and search carefully for the child. And when you find him, come back and tell me so that I can go and worship him, too!"

After this interview the wise men went their way. And the star they had seen in the east guided them to Bethlehem. It went ahead of them and stopped over the place where the child was. When

Reflection

What do Simeon and Anna say about who Jesus is?

What would you share about who you've discovered Jesus to be?

they saw the star, they were filled with joy! They entered the house and saw the child with his mother, Mary, and they bowed down and worshiped him. Then they opened their treasure chests and gave him gifts of gold, frankincense, and myrrh.

When it was time to leave, they returned to their own country by another route, for God had warned them in a dream not to return to Herod.

After the wise men were gone, an angel of the Lord appeared to Joseph in a dream. "Get up! Flee to Egypt with the child and his mother," the angel said. "Stay there until I tell you to return, because Herod is going to search for the child to kill him."

That night Joseph left for Egypt with the child and Mary, his mother, and they stayed there until Herod's death. This fulfilled what the Lord had spoken through the prophet: "I called my Son out of Egypt."

Herod was furious when he realized that the wise men had outwitted him. He sent soldiers to kill all the boys in and around Bethlehem who were two years old and under, based on the wise men's report of the star's first appearance. Herod's brutal action fulfilled what God had spoken through the prophet Jeremiah:

"A cry was heard in Ramah—weeping and great mourning. Rachel weeps for her children, refusing to be comforted, for they are dead."

When Herod died, an angel of the Lord appeared in a dream to Joseph in Egypt. "Get up!" the angel said. "Take the child and his mother back to the land of Israel, because those who were trying to kill the child are dead."

So Joseph got up and returned to the land of Israel with Jesus and his mother. But when he learned that the new ruler of Judea was Herod's son Archelaus, he was afraid to go there. Then, after being warned in a dream, he left for the region of Galilee. So the family went and lived in a town called Nazareth. This fulfilled what the prophets had said: "He will be called a Nazarene."

There the child grew up healthy and strong. He was filled with wisdom, and God's favor was on him.

Two divine births and two divine destinies. At the end of both birth stories we come to the same conclusion: Two strong young men of God are determined to do what God has called them to do.

Every year Jesus' parents went to Jerusalem for the Passover festival. When Jesus was twelve years old, they attended the festival as usual. After the celebration was over, they started home to Nazareth, but Jesus stayed behind in Jerusalem. His parents didn't miss him at first, because they assumed he was among the other travelers. But when he didn't show up that evening, they started looking for him among their relatives and friends.

When they couldn't find him, they went back to Jerusalem to search for him there. Three days later they finally discovered him in the Temple, sitting among the religious teachers, listening to them and asking questions. All who heard him were amazed at his understanding and his answers.

His parents didn't know what to think. "Son," his mother said to him, "why have you done this to us? Your father and I have been frantic, searching for you everywhere."

"But why did you need to search?" he asked. "Didn't you know that I must be in my Father's house?" But they didn't understand what he meant. Then he returned to Nazareth with them and was obedient to them. And his mother stored all these things in her heart.

Jesus grew in wisdom and in stature and in favor with God and all the people.

Reflection

What do you notice about how the wise men sought Jesus?

The wise men worshipped Jesus with gifts and treasures. How will you worship the Lord with your gifts and treasures this year?

We shouldn't interpret Jesus' actions as defiance to His parents. When Mary and Joseph finally find Him, Jesus is the first and "only" twelve-year-old with a perfectly good explanation. How could they have known that their pre-teen was busy instructing the Temple priests? To their credit, they accept that Jesus has been given instructions from His "heavenly" Father. And they also know that Jesus isn't a typical twelve-year-old boy. He's a young man who has already figured out who He is and has been preparing for the mission He was sent to accomplish.

Scripture References

Luke 1–2; 3:23–38; John 1:1–18; Matthew 1–2

First Year of His Mission

Travels in the First Year of His Mission

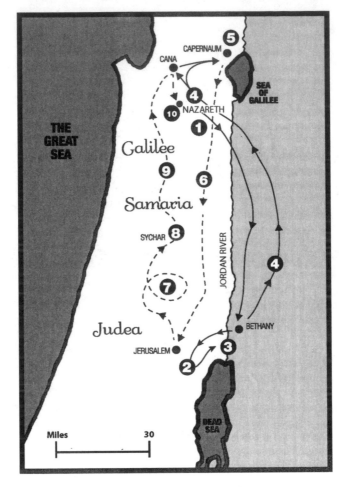

1. From Galilee to the Jordan River.

2. From the Jordan River to the wilderness of Judea.

3. From the wilderness to Bethany.

4. From Bethany to Cana.

5. From Cana to Capernaum.

6. From Capernaum to Jerusalem for the Passover.

7. From Jerusalem to the Judean countryside.

8. From the Judean countryside to Jacob's well at Sychar.

9. From Samaria to Cana in Galilee.

10. From Cana to Nazareth.

Chapter 2

Jesus' Mission Begins

Jesus' preparation is coming to an end and the time is coming to launch the ministry that will revo-lutionize history! It won't be a celebrity life; it will be tough. He will be tested by Satan in the wilderness and led to confront the establishment. But He also reveals His power by changing water to wine, and even more impressively, He reveals His true purpose, to redeem people. But first, Jesus must be introduced to the world. How will God accomplish this? As prophesied years ago, God's surprising choice is Jesus' cousin from Chapter One, who is now a well-known eccentric prophet named John the Baptist.

This is the Good News[5] about Jesus the Messiah, the Son of God.

It was now the fifteenth year of the reign of Tiberius, the Roman emperor. Pontius Pilate was governor over Judea; Herod Antipas was ruler over Galilee; his brother Philip was ruler over Iturea and Traconitis; Lysanias was ruler over Abilene. Annas and Caiaphas were the high priests.[6] At this time a

---

[5] **Good News:** This could also be translated as "Gospel." It is the good news that Jesus came to reconcile humanity to God. Through His death and resurrection, we can enter into a relationship with God and walk in a new way of life.

[6] This sentence and ones like it show us the historical context of the life and times of Jesus. Since Rome ruled over the Jewish people, Luke describes the Roman and Jewish structure of authority. Regarding Rome, he tells us which emperor was in power; Pontius Pilate was the procurator (governor) of Judea; Herod was the tetrarch or "ruler" over

message from God came to John son of Zechariah, who was living out in the wilderness.

In those days John the Baptist came to the Judean wilderness and began preaching. Then John went from place to place on both sides of the Jordan River, preaching that people should be baptized[7] to show that they had repented of their sins and turned to God to be forgiven. His message was, "Repent of your sins and turn to God, for the Kingdom of Heaven is near."

Isaiah had spoken of John when he said,

"Look, I am sending my messenger ahead of you, and he will prepare your way. He is a voice shouting in the wilderness, 'Prepare the way for the LORD's coming! Clear the road for him! The valleys will be filled, and the mountains and hills made level. The curves will be straightened, and the rough places made smooth! And then all people will see the salvation sent from God.' "

John's clothes were woven from coarse camel hair, and he wore a leather belt around his waist. For

---

Galilee; and his brother Philip ruled over four other regions. In regard to the Jewish power structure, Annas was the former high priest, but like former American presidents, was still considered "Mr. High Priest"; while his son-in-law Caiaphas was the current ruling high priest.

[7] **baptized**: The act of being immersed in water that demonstrates leaving your former way of life and embracing the new way of life with Jesus. One who has believed, confessed and repented should be baptized, in a timely act of obedience, in following Jesus.

food he ate locusts and wild honey. People from Jerusalem and from all of Judea and all over the Jordan Valley went out to see and hear John. And when they confessed their sins, he baptized them in the Jordan River.

But when he saw many Pharisees[8] and Sadducees[9] coming to watch him baptize, he denounced them: "You brood of snakes! Who warned you to flee God's coming wrath? Prove by the way you live that you have repented[10] from your sins and turned to God. Don't just say to each other, 'We're safe—for we are descendants of Abraham.' That means nothing, for I tell you, God can create children of Abraham from these very stones. Even now the ax of God's judgment is poised, ready to sever the roots of the trees. Yes, every tree that does not produce good fruit will be chopped down and thrown into the fire."

The crowds asked, "What should we do?"

---

[8] **Pharisees**: The most powerful group of religious authorities within Judaism. The Pharisees' main emphasis was on their interpretation of God's laws, and they often challenged Jesus based on what they perceived to be violations of these laws.

[9] **Sadducees**: An upper class of Jewish leaders who oversaw the Temple administration. As a group, they denied the resurrection of the dead, the existence of spirits, and the obligation of oral tradition, emphasizing acceptance of the written law alone.

[10] **repented**: Repentance literally means "a change of mind" and signifies a total change in the direction of one's life. Since the Hebrew concept of the mind was not only intellectual, but also encompassed what we label as heart, attitude, motivations, and will, a modern definition would be "a total change of mind and heart leading to action."

John replied, "If you have two shirts, give one to the poor. If you have food, share it with those who are hungry."

Even corrupt tax collectors came to be baptized and asked, "Teacher, what should we do?"

He replied, "Collect no more taxes than the government requires."

"What should we do?" asked some soldiers.

John replied, "Don't extort money or make false accusations. And be content with your pay."

Everyone was expecting the Messiah to come soon, and they were eager to know whether John might be the Messiah. John answered their questions by saying, "I baptize with water those who repent of their sins and turn to God. But someone is coming soon who is greater than I am—so much greater that I'm not even worthy to be his slave and untie the strap of his sandals. He will baptize you with the Holy Spirit and with fire. He is ready to separate the chaff from the wheat with his winnowing fork. Then he will clean up the threshing area, gathering the wheat into his barn but burning the chaff with never-ending fire." John used many such warnings as he announced the Good News to the people.

John's message of repentance challenges people to turn away from their sin and to change. Once convicted of sin, people ask what they need to do. John's images are very concrete in proving sincere repentance has taken place. People are so moved they begin to wonder if, even hope that, John might be the Messiah. But John understands his role well. By pointing away from himself, he is doing what God sent him to do: prepare people to

Reflection

How did John the Baptist encourage different groups of people to respond to his message? What was his message?

How do you recognize repentance in your own life?

receive what Jesus has to offer. That's when the true Messiah shows up!

Then Jesus went from Galilee to the Jordan River to be baptized by John. But John tried to talk him out of it. "I am the one who needs to be baptized by you," he said, "so why are you coming to me?"

But Jesus said, "It should be done, for we must carry out all that God requires." So John agreed to baptize him.

One day when the crowds were being baptized, Jesus himself was baptized. Jesus came up out of the water and as he was praying, the heavens opened, and the Holy Spirit, in bodily form, descended on him like a dove. And a voice from heaven said, "You are my dearly loved Son, and you bring me great joy."

Jesus was about thirty years old when he began his public ministry.

Then Jesus, full of the Holy Spirit, returned from the Jordan River. He was led by the Spirit into the wilderness to be tempted there by the devil. For forty days and forty nights he fasted and became very hungry. He was out among the wild animals.

During that time the devil came and said to him, "If you are the Son of God, tell these stones to become loaves of bread."

But Jesus told him, "No! The Scriptures say,

'People do not live by bread alone, but by every word that comes from the mouth of God.' "

Then the devil took him to the holy city, Jerusalem, to the highest point of the Temple, and said, "If you are the Son of God, jump off! For the Scriptures say,

'He will order his angels to protect you. And they will hold you up with their hands so you won't even hurt your foot on a stone.' "

Jesus responded, "The Scriptures also say,

'You must not test the LORD your God.' "

Then the devil took him up and revealed to him all the kingdoms of the world in a moment of time. "I will give you the glory of these kingdoms and authority over them," the devil said, "because they are mine to give to anyone I please. I will give it all to you if you will worship me."

"Get out of here, Satan," Jesus told him. "For the Scriptures say,

'You must worship the LORD your God and serve only him.' "

When the devil had finished tempting Jesus, he left him until the next opportunity came, and angels took care of Jesus.

After weeks without anything to eat in this harsh and barren wilderness, one can only imagine how badly Jesus wants to eat. Sleep is also in short supply since Jesus uses a rock for a pillow and sand for a bed. That's when Satan tempts Jesus to take the shortcut to power. Three times Jesus resists Satan by quoting the truth of Scripture. Passing this major test in the wilderness confirms His identity as the true Messiah. God's plan was for Jesus to be the King who came to serve His people, not be served—ultimately laying down His life for His people.

But that will come later, for now John the Baptist will once and for all turn the spotlight away from himself and onto Jesus.

This was John's testimony when the Jewish leaders sent priests and Temple assistants from Jerusalem to ask John, "Who are you?" He came right out and said, "I am not the Messiah."

"Well then, who are you?" they asked. "Are you Elijah?"

"No," he replied.

"Are you the Prophet we are expecting?"

"No."

"Then who are you? We need an answer for those who sent us. What do you have to say about yourself?"

John replied in the words of the prophet Isaiah:

"I am a voice shouting in the wilderness, 'Clear the way for the LORD's coming!' "

Then the Pharisees who had been sent asked him, "If you aren't the Messiah or Elijah or the Prophet, what right do you have to baptize?"

John told them, "I baptize with water, but right here in the crowd is someone you do not recognize. Though his ministry follows mine, I'm not even worthy to be his slave and untie the straps of his sandal."

This encounter took place in Bethany, an area east of the Jordan River, where John was baptizing.

⌘

Reflection

The next day John saw Jesus coming toward him and said, "Look! The Lamb of God who takes away the sin of the world! He is the one I was talking about when I said, 'A man is coming after me who is far greater than I am, for he existed long before me.' I did not recognize him as the Messiah, but I have been baptizing with water so that he might be revealed to Israel."

Then John testified, "I saw the Holy Spirit descending like a dove from heaven and resting upon him. I didn't know he was the one, but when God sent me to baptize with water, he told me, 'The one on whom you see the Spirit descend and rest is the one who will baptize with the Holy Spirit.' I saw this happen to Jesus, so I testify that he is the Chosen One of God."

After His baptism and wilderness testing, Jesus is ready to go public with His message and ministry. What will be His main strategy for reaching the world? Even though He heals many and teaches huge crowds, Jesus' message will eventually be taken to all nations through a few carefully chosen men—the disciples. God has already determined who they will be; now it's just a matter of Jesus' inviting them to join Him.

The following day John was again standing with two of his disciples. As Jesus walked by, John looked at him and declared, "Look! There is the Lamb of God!" When John's two disciples heard this, they followed Jesus.

Jesus looked around and saw them following. "What do you want?" he asked them.

Jesus and John are both challenged regarding who they are. How did each of them respond?

How do you handle temptation when it comes?

They replied, "Rabbi" (which means "Teacher"), "where are you staying?"

"Come and see," he said. It was about four o'clock in the afternoon when they went with him to the place where he was staying, and they remained with him the rest of the day.

Andrew, Simon Peter's brother, was one of these men who heard what John said and then followed Jesus. Andrew went to find his brother, Simon, and told him, "We have found the Messiah" (which means "Christ").

Then Andrew brought Simon to meet Jesus. Looking intently at Simon, Jesus said, "Your name is Simon, son of John—but you will be called Cephas" (which means "Peter").

The next day Jesus decided to go to Galilee. He found Philip and said to him, "Come, follow me." Philip was from Bethsaida, Andrew and Peter's hometown.

Philip went to look for Nathanael and told him, "We have found the very person Moses and the prophets wrote about! His name is Jesus, the son of Joseph from Nazareth."

"Nazareth!" exclaimed Nathanael. "Can anything good come from Nazareth?"

"Come and see for yourself," Philip replied.

As they approached, Jesus said, "Now here is a genuine son of Israel—a man of complete integrity."

"How do you know about me?" Nathanael asked.

Jesus replied, "I could see you under the fig tree before Philip found you."

Then Nathanael exclaimed, "Rabbi, you are the Son of God—the King of Israel!"

Jesus asked him, "Do you believe this just because I told you I had seen you under the fig tree? You will see greater things than this." Then he said, "I tell you the truth, you will all see heaven open and the angels of God going up and down on the Son of Man, the one who is the stairway between heaven and earth."

The next day there was a wedding celebration in the village of Cana in Galilee. Jesus' mother was there, and Jesus and his disciples were also invited to the celebration. The wine supply ran out during the festivities, so Jesus' mother told him, "They have no more wine."

"Dear woman, that's not our problem," Jesus replied. "My time has not yet come."

But his mother told the servants, "Do whatever he tells you."

Standing nearby were six stone water jars, used for Jewish ceremonial washing. Each could hold twenty to thirty gallons. Jesus told the servants, "Fill the jars with water." When the jars had been filled, he said, "Now dip some out, and take it to the master of ceremonies." So the servants followed his instructions.

When the master of ceremonies tasted the water that was now wine, not knowing where it had come from (though, of course, the servants knew), he called the bridegroom over. "A host always serves the best wine first," he said. "Then, when everyone has had a lot to drink, he brings out the less expensive wine. But you have kept the best until now!"

This miraculous sign at Cana in Galilee was the first time Jesus revealed his glory. And his disciples believed in him.

After the wedding he went to Capernaum for a few days with his mother, his brothers, and his disciples.

At Cana, Jesus performs the first of many miracles. In doing so He reveals both His power and His compassion. Jewish weddings could often last seven days and as you can imagine, the family wanted it to be a celebration to remember. Running out of wine would be a disaster no family would wish to remember. So Jesus not only does the impossible in changing the water to wine, but He makes wine so high in quality that no one can believe it was saved until the end of the wedding. For wine buffs, it may be easy to appreciate the difference between a cheap, watered down wine and a full-body quality wine. For those who don't relate to wine, it would be like going to a wedding reception with Jesus where they run out of little ham sandwiches, and Jesus makes a tender prime rib and a fresh shrimp buffet in their place. This sign is a subtle message about eternal life with Jesus: Hang with Jesus and the best is yet to come!

Jesus' first confrontation is equally remarkable. As He enters the Temple, what He discovers is not prayer and worship, but the commercialization of religion. Generosity to those seeking a relationship with God has been replaced with greed, and those responsible are the very ones who should know better. So what does Jesus do?

It was nearly time for the Jewish Passover celebration, so Jesus went to Jerusalem. In the Temple area he saw merchants selling cattle, sheep, and doves for sacrifices; he also saw dealers at tables exchanging foreign money. Jesus made a whip from some ropes and chased them all out of the Temple. He drove out the sheep and cattle, scattered the money changers' coins over the floor, and turned over their tables. Then, going over to the people who sold doves, he told them, "Get these things out of here. Stop turning my Father's house into a marketplace!"

Then his disciples remembered this prophecy from the Scriptures: "Passion for God's house will consume me."

But the Jewish leaders demanded, "What are you doing? If God gave you authority to do this, show us a miraculous sign to prove it."

"All right," Jesus replied. "Destroy this temple, and in three days I will raise it up."

"What!" they exclaimed. "It has taken forty-six years to build this Temple, and you can rebuild it in three days?" But when Jesus said "this temple," he meant his own body. After he was raised from the dead, his disciples remembered he had said this, and they believed both the Scriptures and what Jesus had said.

Because of the miraculous signs Jesus did in Jerusalem at the Passover celebration, many began to trust in him. But Jesus didn't trust them, because he knew human nature. No one needed to tell him what mankind is really like.

Reflection

What happened when John the Baptist, Andrew or Philip discovered who Jesus was?

What helps you believe Jesus is who he says he is? How are you helping prepare other people to encounter Jesus?

There was a man named Nicodemus, a Jewish religious leader who was a Pharisee. After dark one evening, he came to speak with Jesus. "Rabbi," he said, "we all know that God has sent you to teach us. Your miraculous signs are evidence that God is with you."

Jesus replied, "I tell you the truth, unless you are born again, you cannot see the Kingdom of God."

"What do you mean?" exclaimed Nicodemus. "How can an old man go back into his mother's womb and be born again?" Jesus replied, "I assure you, no one can enter the Kingdom of God without being born of water and the Spirit. Humans can reproduce only human life, but the Holy Spirit gives birth to spiritual life. So don't be surprised when I say, 'You must be born again.'   The wind blows wherever it wants. Just as you can hear the wind but can't tell where it comes from or where it is going, so you can't explain how people are born of the Spirit."

"How are these things possible?" Nicodemus asked.

Jesus replied, "You are a respected Jewish teacher, and yet you don't understand these things? I assure you, we tell you what we know and have seen, and yet you won't believe our testimony. But if you don't believe me when I tell you about earthly things, how can you possibly believe if I tell you about heavenly things? No one has ever gone to heaven and returned. But the Son of Man has come down from heaven. And as Moses lifted up the bronze snake on a pole in the wilderness, so the Son of Man must be lifted up, so that everyone who believes in him will have eternal life.

"For God loved the world so much that he gave his one and only Son, so that everyone who believes in him will not perish but have eternal life. God sent his Son into the world not to judge the world, but to save the world through him.

"There is no judgment against anyone who believes in him. But anyone who does not believe in him has already been judged for not believing in God's one and only Son. And the judgment is based on this fact: God's light came into the world, but people loved the darkness more than the light, for their actions were evil. All who do evil hate the light and refuse to go near it for fear their sins will be exposed. But those who do what is right come to the light so others can see that they are doing what God wants."

Then Jesus and his disciples left Jerusalem and went into the Judean countryside. Jesus spent some time with them there, baptizing people.

At this time John the Baptist was baptizing at Aenon, near Salim, because there was plenty of water there; and people kept coming to him for baptism. (This was before John was thrown into prison.) A debate broke out between John's disciples and a certain Jew over ceremonial cleansing. So John's disciples came to him and said, "Rabbi, the man you met on the other side of the Jordan River, the one you identified as the Messiah, is also baptizing people. And every-body is going to him instead of coming to us."

John replied, "No one can receive anything unless God gives it from heaven. You yourselves know how plainly I told you, 'I am not the Messiah. I am only here to prepare the way for him.' It is the bridegroom who marries the bride, and the best man is simply glad to stand with him and hear his vows. Therefore, I am filled with joy at his success. He must become greater and greater, and I must become less and less.

"He has come from above and is greater than anyone else. We are of the earth, and we speak of earthly things, but he has come from heaven and is greater than anyone else. He testifies about what he has seen and heard, but how few believe what he tells them! Anyone who accepts his testimony can affirm that God is true. For he is sent by God. He speaks God's words, for God gives him the Spirit without limit. The Father loves his Son and has put everything into his hands. And anyone who believes in God's Son has eternal life. Anyone who doesn't obey the Son will never experience eternal life but remains under God's angry judgment."

Nicodemus is a religious seeker who learns that entering God's Kingdom is not about religion but "rebirth" through Jesus. In a few days, as Jesus passes through Samaria, He will be approached by a different kind of seeker, a sinful woman. Most devout Jews rarely passed through Samaria because of their prejudice toward the Samaritans. Jesus, however, travels through Samaria in order to avoid a conflict with both the Pharisees and Herod. Both of these disputes revolve around John the Baptist, who is still confronting sin in people's lives. This time John calls out Herod, who uses his power to throw John in prison. Jesus will face Herod one day, but His time for that has not yet come. Besides, Jesus has a divine appointment in Samaria that He must keep.

John[11] also publicly criticized Herod Antipas, the ruler of Galilee, for marrying Herodias, his brother's wife, and for many other wrongs he had done. So Herod put John in prison, adding this sin to his many others.

Jesus heard that John had been arrested, and Jesus also[12] knew the Pharisees had heard that he was baptizing and making more disciples than John (though Jesus himself didn't baptize them—his disciples did). So he left Judea and returned to Galilee, filled with the Holy Spirit's power.

He had to go through Samaria[13] on the way. Eventually he came to the Samaritan village of Sychar, near the field that Jacob gave to his son Joseph. Jacob's well was there; and Jesus, tired from the long walk, sat wearily beside the well about

---

[11] **John**: Jesus' cousin John the Baptist.

[12] **also**: This word is added to provide a smooth harmony between Matthew's Gospel and John's Gospel.

[13] **Samaria**: Samaria was a region located approximately 35 miles north of Jerusalem on the west side of the Jordan River. The Samaritan people were descendants of the surviving Israelites of the Northern Kingdom who intermarried with the newly imported alien population after the fall of Samaria in 722 B.C. There was a clear rift between Samaritans and Jews beginning in Nehemiah's time, but it was sealed when a Samaritan temple was built on Mount Gerizim, overlooking Shechem (John 4:20). The temple was destroyed by the Jewish king Hyrcanus in 128 B.C. The Samaritans worshiped the same God as the Jews did and even used the Five Books of Moses (Genesis–Deuteronomy) as their authority. Like the Jews, they awaited the coming of a prophet like Moses, a Messiah. Jewish hatred and disdain for the Samaritans sprang more from historical and racial tensions than from any fundamental differences of religion.

Reflection

What was Nicodemus looking for when he approached Jesus? What did he find?

If you had an opportunity like Nicodemus what would you discuss with Jesus?

noontime. Soon a Samaritan woman came to draw water, and Jesus said to her, "Please give me a drink." He was alone at the time because his disciples had gone into the village to buy some food.

The woman was surprised, for Jews refuse to have anything to do with Samaritans. She said to Jesus, "You are a Jew, and I am a Samaritan woman. Why are you asking me for a drink?"

Jesus replied, "If you only knew the gift God has for you and who you are speaking to, you would ask me, and I would give you living water."

"But sir, you don't have a rope or a bucket," she said, "and this well is very deep. Where would you get this living water? And besides, do you think you're greater than our ancestor Jacob, who gave us this well? How can you offer better water than he and his sons and his animals enjoyed?"

Jesus replied, "Anyone who drinks this water will soon become thirsty again. But those who drink the water I give will never be thirsty again. It becomes a fresh, bubbling spring within them, giving them eternal life."

"Please, sir," the woman said, "give me this water! Then I'll never be thirsty again, and I won't have to come here to get water."

"Go and get your husband," Jesus told her.

"I don't have a husband," the woman replied.

Jesus said, "You're right! You don't have a husband— for you have had five husbands, and you aren't even married to the man you're living with now. You certainly spoke the truth!"

"Sir," the woman said, "you must be a prophet. So tell me, why is it that you Jews insist that Jerusalem is the only place of worship, while we

Samaritans claim it is here at Mount Gerizim, where our ancestors worshiped?"

Jesus replied, "Believe me, dear woman, the time is coming when it will no longer matter whether you worship the Father on this mountain or in Jerusalem. You Samaritans know very little about the one you worship, while we Jews know all about him, for salvation comes through the Jews. But the time is coming—indeed it's here now—when true worshipers will worship the Father in spirit and in truth. The Father is looking for those who will worship him that way. For God is Spirit, so those who worship him must worship in spirit and in truth."

The woman said, "I know the Messiah is coming—the one who is called Christ. When he comes, he will explain everything to us."

Then Jesus told her, "I AM the Messiah!"

Just then his disciples came back. They were shocked to find him talking to a woman, but none of them had the nerve to ask, "What do you want with her?" or "Why are you talking to her?" The woman left her water jar beside the well and ran back to the village, telling everyone, "Come and see a man who told me everything I ever did! Could he possibly be the Messiah?" So the people came streaming from the village to see him.

Meanwhile, the disciples were urging Jesus, "Rabbi, eat something."

But Jesus replied, "I have a kind of food you know nothing about."

"Did someone bring him food while we were gone?" the disciples asked each other.

Then Jesus explained: "My nourishment comes
from doing the will of God, who sent me, and from
finishing his work. You know the saying, 'Four
months between planting and harvest.' But I say,
wake up and look around. The fields are already ripe
for harvest. The harvesters are paid good wages, and
the fruit they harvest is people brought to eternal
life. What joy awaits both the planter and the
harvester alike! You know the saying, 'One plants
and another harvests.' And it's true. I sent you to
harvest where you didn't plant; others had already
done the work, and now you will get to gather the
harvest."

Many Samaritans from the village believed in
Jesus because the woman had said, "He told me
everything I ever did!" When they came out to see
him, they begged him to stay in their village. So he
stayed for two days, long enough for many more to
hear his message and believe. Then they said to the
woman, "Now we believe, not just because of what
you told us, but because we have heard him
ourselves. Now we know that he is indeed the Savior
of the world."

> *Fresh cold water when we're parched is to our*
> *bodies what Jesus is to our lives. The difference,*
> *however, is Jesus brings eternal satisfaction. This*
> *is what the Samaritan woman learns from her*
> *encounter with Jesus. Her amazing testimony is so*
> *contagious that many in the town of Sychar believe*
> *and even convince Jesus to stay two extra days.*
> *During those two days, even more people come to*
> *faith. How deep was their faith? How mature?*
> *We don't know but Jesus shows over and over*
> *again that it doesn't take Him long to change a*
> *heart that is open. Like He did in Samaria,*

Jesus will continue to break down the walls of race, gender, and sin in order to accomplish His mission—to seek and save the lost.

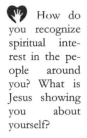 What keeps the woman engaged in the conversation with Jesus?

Scripture References

Mark 1:1–14; Luke 3:1–23; 4:1–13; Matthew 3:1—4:12; John 1:19—4:42

How do you recognize spiritual interest in the people around you? What is Jesus showing you about yourself?

Chapter 3

Jesus Calls Disciples to Follow Him

Even though Jesus has spent only two days in Samaria, countless lives are forever changed. After being away from His homeland for about a year, Jesus returns to the beautiful region of Galilee to continue His miraculous ministry and calls on some followers to be His disciples. The next eighteen months are often considered His "Galilean Ministry," because in Galilee He performs most of His well-known miracles and proclaims much of His core teaching.

At the end of the two days, Jesus went on to Galilee. He himself had said that a prophet is not honored in his own hometown. Yet the Galileans welcomed him, for they had been in Jerusalem at the Passover celebration and had seen everything he did there.

From then on Jesus began to preach God's Good News. "The time promised by God has come at last!" he announced. "The Kingdom of God is near! Repent of your sins and believe the Good News!"

Reports about him spread quickly through the whole region. He taught regularly in their synagogues and was praised by everyone.

As he traveled through Galilee, he came to Cana, where he had turned the water into wine. There was a government official in nearby Capernaum whose son was very sick. When he heard that Jesus had come from Judea to Galilee, he went and begged Jesus to come to Capernaum to heal his son, who was about to die.

Jesus asked, "Will you never believe in me unless you see miraculous signs and wonders?"

The official pleaded, "Lord, please come now before my little boy dies."

Then Jesus told him, "Go back home. Your son will live!" And the man believed what Jesus said and started home.

While the man was on his way, some of his servants met him with the news that his son was alive and well. He asked them when the boy had begun to get better, and they replied, "Yesterday afternoon at one o'clock his fever suddenly disappeared!" Then the father realized that that was the very time Jesus had told him, "Your son will live." And he and his entire household believed in Jesus. This was the second miraculous sign Jesus did in Galilee after coming from Judea.

> *Because of His miraculous works and revolutionary approach to God's Word, Jesus is quickly gaining quite a following throughout the region. Now Jesus returns to his hometown where people watched Jesus grow up, play with His friends, attend school, learn His father's trade, and work alongside others in neighboring villages as a grown man. Now things are different, and it's up to each person to decide if they will accept His message or not.*

When he came to the village of Nazareth, his boyhood home, he went as usual to the synagogue on the Sabbath and stood up to read the Scriptures. The scroll of Isaiah the prophet was handed to him. He unrolled the scroll and found the place where this was written:

"The Spirit of the LORD is upon me, for he has anointed me to bring Good News to the poor. He has sent me to proclaim that captives will be released, that the blind will see, that the oppressed will be set free, and that the time of the LORD's favor has come."

He rolled up the scroll, handed it back to the attendant, and sat down. All eyes in the synagogue looked at him intently. Then he began to speak to them. "The Scripture you've just heard has been fulfilled this very day!"

Everyone spoke well of him and was amazed by the gracious words that came from his lips. "How can this be?" they asked. "Isn't this Joseph's son?"

Then he said, "You will undoubtedly quote me this proverb: 'Physician, heal yourself'—meaning, 'Do miracles here in your hometown like those you did in Capernaum.' But I tell you the truth, no prophet is accepted in his own hometown.

"Certainly there were many needy widows in Israel in Elijah's time, when the heavens were closed for three and a half years, and a severe famine devastated the land. Yet Elijah was not sent to any of them. He was sent instead to a foreigner—a widow of Zarephath in the land of Sidon. And there were many lepers in Israel in the time of the prophet Elisha, but the only one healed was Naaman, a Syrian."

When they heard this, the people in the synagogue were furious. Jumping up, they mobbed him and forced him to the edge of the hill on which the town was built. They intended to push him over the cliff, but he passed right through the crowd and went on his way.

Then Jesus moved to Capernaum, beside the Sea of Galilee, in the region of Zebulun and Naphtali. This fulfilled what God said through the prophet Isaiah:

> "In the land of Zebulun and of Naphtali, beside the sea, beyond the Jordan River, in Galilee where so many Gentiles live, the people who sat in darkness have seen a great light. And for those who lived in the land where death casts its shadow, a light has shined."

Reflection

What was the man's response to Jesus' claim that his son would live?

Where do you struggle with believing Jesus' claims to be true right now in your own life?

One day as Jesus was walking along the shore of the Sea of Galilee, he saw two brothers—Simon, also called Peter, and Andrew—throwing a net into the water, for they fished for a living.

As Jesus was preaching on the shore of the Sea of Galilee, great crowds pressed in on him to listen to the word of God. He noticed two empty boats at the water's edge, for the fishermen had left them and were washing their nets. Stepping into one of the boats, Jesus asked Simon, its owner, to push it out into the water. So he sat in the boat and taught the crowds from there.

When he had finished speaking, he said to Simon, "Now go out where it is deeper, and let down your nets to catch some fish."

"Master," Simon replied, "we worked hard all last night and didn't catch a thing. But if you say so,

I'll let the nets down again." And this time their nets were so full of fish they began to tear! A shout for help brought their partners in the other boat, and soon both boats were filled with fish and on the verge of sinking.

When Simon Peter realized what had happened, he fell to his knees before Jesus and said, "Oh, Lord, please leave me—I'm too much of a sinner to be around you," for he was awestruck by the number of fish they had caught.

Jesus replied to Simon, "Don't be afraid! Come, follow me, and I will show you how to fish for people!" And as soon as they landed, they left everything and followed Jesus.

A little farther up the shore he saw two other brothers, James and John, sitting in a boat with their father, Zebedee, repairing their nets. And he called them to come, too. They immediately followed him, leaving their father, Zebedee, in the boat with the hired men.

Jesus and his companions went to the town of Capernaum. When the Sabbath day came, he went into the synagogue and began to teach. The people were amazed at his teaching, for he taught with real authority—quite unlike the teachers of religious law.

Once when he was in the synagogue, a man possessed by a demon—an evil spirit—began shouting at Jesus, "Go away! Why are you interfering with us, Jesus of Nazareth? Have you come to destroy us? I know who you are—the Holy One of God!"

Jesus cut him short. "Be quiet! Come out of the man," he ordered. At that, the demon screamed, threw the man to the floor into a convulsion as the crowd watched; then it came out of him without hurting him further.

Amazement gripped the audience, and they began to discuss what had happened. "What sort of new teaching is this?" they asked excitedly. "It has such authority! Even evil spirits obey his orders!" The news about Jesus spread quickly throughout the entire region of Galilee.

After Jesus left the synagogue with James and John, they went to Simon and Andrew's home. Now Simon's mother-in-law was sick in bed with a high fever. They told Jesus about her right away. So he went to her bedside, rebuked the fever, took her by the hand, and helped her sit up. Then the fever left her, and she prepared a meal for them.

As the sun went down that evening, people throughout the village brought sick family members to Jesus. No matter what their diseases were, the touch of his hand healed every one. Many were possessed by demons; and the demons came out at his command, shouting, "You are the Son of God!" But because they knew he was the Messiah, he rebuked them and refused to let them speak.

This fulfilled the word of the Lord through the prophet Isaiah, who said,

> "He took our sicknesses and removed our diseases."

Before daybreak the next morning, Jesus got up and went out to an isolated place to pray. Later Simon and the crowds went out to find him. When they found him, they said, "Everyone is looking for you." They begged him not to leave them. But he replied, "I must preach the Good News of the

Reflection

🧠 What do you notice about Jesus' interactions with people?

💗 What are some situations you need Jesus to us his authority to speak chaos into order in your life, your family, your work place, or your community?

Kingdom of God in other towns, too, because that is why I was sent."

⌘

Jesus traveled throughout the region of Galilee, teaching in the synagogues and announcing the Good News about the Kingdom. And he healed every kind of disease and illness. News about him spread as far as Syria, and people soon began bringing to him all who were sick. And whatever their sickness or disease, or if they were demon-possessed or epileptic or paralyzed—he healed them all. Large crowds followed him wherever he went—people from Galilee, the Ten Towns, Jerusalem, from all over Judea, and from east of the Jordan River.

In one of the villages, Jesus met a man with an advanced case of leprosy. When the man saw Jesus, he bowed with his face to the ground, begging to be healed. "Lord," he said, "if you are willing, you can heal me and make me clean."

Moved with compassion, Jesus reached out and touched him. "I am willing," he said. "Be healed!" Instantly the leprosy disappeared, and the man was healed. Then Jesus sent him on his way with a stern warning: "Don't tell anyone about this. Instead, go to the priest and let him examine you. Take along the offering required in the law of Moses for those who have been healed of leprosy. This will be a public testimony that you have been cleansed."

But the man went and spread the word, proclaiming to everyone what had happened. As a result, large crowds soon surrounded Jesus, and he couldn't publicly enter a town anywhere. He had to stay out in the secluded places, but people from everywhere kept coming to him to hear him preach and to be healed of their diseases. But Jesus often withdrew to the wilderness for prayer.

Just as Jesus teaches His followers about the Kingdom of God and demonstrates what the Kingdom of God is like by healing the sick, the Pharisees are training disciples of their own (one of whom would, in a grand display of irony, eventually become the apostle Paul). Because Jesus' popularity is quickly growing, the Pharisees put together a group to examine whether Jesus' teachings are positive or negative. We've seen Jesus confront the religious leaders; now the Pharisees will oppose Jesus for the first time.

When Jesus returned to Capernaum several days later, the news spread quickly that he was back home. Soon the house where he was staying was so packed with visitors that there was no more room, even outside the door.

While he was preaching God's word to them, some Pharisees and teachers of religious law were sitting nearby. (It seemed that these men showed up from every village in all Galilee and Judea, as well as from Jerusalem.) And the Lord's healing power was strongly with Jesus.

Four men came carrying a paralyzed man on a sleeping mat. They tried to take him inside to Jesus, but they couldn't reach him because of the crowd. So they went up to the roof and dug a hole through the roof above his head. Then they lowered the sick man on his mat down into the crowd, right in front of Jesus. Seeing their faith, Jesus said to the man, "Young man, your sins are forgiven."

But the Pharisees and teachers of religious law said to themselves, "Who does he think he is? That's blasphemy! Only God can forgive sins!"

Jesus knew immediately what they were thinking, so he asked them, "Why do you question this in your hearts? Is it easier to say to the paralyzed man 'Your sins are forgiven,' or 'Stand up, pick up your mat, and walk'? So I will prove to you that the Son of Man has the authority on earth to forgive sins." Then Jesus turned to the paralyzed man and said, "Stand up, pick up your mat, and go home!"

And immediately, as everyone watched, the man jumped up, picked up his mat, and went home praising God. Everyone was gripped with great wonder and awe, and they praised God for sending a man with such great authority, exclaiming, "We have seen amazing things today!"

Then Jesus went out to the lakeshore again and taught the crowds that were coming to him. As he walked along, he saw Levi[14] son of Alphaeus sitting at his tax collector's booth. "Follow me and be my disciple," Jesus said to him. So Levi got up, left everything, and followed him.

Later, Levi held a banquet in his home with Jesus as the guest of honor. Many of Levi's fellow tax collectors and other disreputable sinners also ate with them. (There were many people of this kind among Jesus' followers.) But the Pharisees and their teachers of religious law complained bitterly to Jesus' disciples, "Why do you eat and drink with such scum?"

---

[14] **Levi**: Also called Matthew; wrote the Gospel of Matthew.

When Jesus heard this, he told them, "Healthy people don't need a doctor—sick people do." Then he added, "Now go and learn the meaning of this Scripture: 'I want you to show mercy, not offer sacrifices.' For I have come to call not those who think they are righteous, but those who know they are sinners."

Once when John's disciples and the Pharisees were fasting, some people came to Jesus and asked, "Why don't your disciples fast[15] like John's disciples and the Pharisees do?"

Jesus replied, "Do wedding guests fast while celebrating with the groom? Of course not. They can't fast while the groom is with them. But someday the groom will be taken away from them, and then they will fast."

Then Jesus gave them this illustration: "No one tears a piece of cloth from a new garment and uses it to patch an old garment. For then the new garment would be ruined, and the new patch wouldn't even match the old garment.

"And no one puts new wine into old wineskins. For the new wine would burst the wineskins, spilling the wine and ruining the skins. New wine must be

---

[15] **fast**: Often Jesus didn't seem religious enough for the Pharisees, but that is because He had a different kind of religion in mind. Jewish law only required fasting once a year on the Day of Atonement, but the Pharisees and teachers of the law added several more fasts throughout the year in their own writings called "The Talmud." Jesus often ignored the Talmud and thereby looked religiously "loose" in the eyes of the Pharisees.

Reflection

What did Jesus see that caused him to heal the man on the mat?

How are you using your faith to help carry people to Jesus?

Reflection

 What are people considering to be maturity?

What are you coming to understand about Jesus' way of life?

stored in new wineskins. But no one who drinks the old wine seems to want the new wine. 'The old is just fine,' they say." Jesus' ministry is now well established and people begin to choose sides. His teaching is a new way of living that offers true freedom and complete healing, not through our own works but through God's grace.

Scripture References

John 4:43–54; Mark 1:14–22; Luke 4:14–5:39; Matthew 4:13–25; 8:2–4, 14–17; 9:1–17

Second Year of His Mission

Travels in the Second Year of His Mission

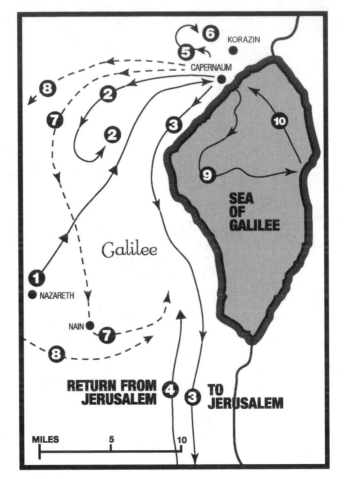

1. From Nazareth to Capernaum.

2. The tour of Galilee and return to Capernaum.

3. From Capernaum to Jerusalem for the Passover.

4. From Jerusalem to Capernaum.

5. From Capernaum to the Mount of Beatitudes.

6. The return from the Mount of Beatitudes to Capernaum.

7. From Capernaum, through Galilee and return.

8. From Capernaum, third tour of Galilee.

9. From Capernaum to the region of the Gerasenes.

10. From the region of the Gerasenes to Capernaum.

Chapter 4

Jesus' Revolutionary Teaching

*So the revolution has begun! We have seen that
Jesus is so shockingly different that He both
amazes and perplexes everyone He encounters. He
claims to be righteous yet hangs out with sinners.
He claims to love God but breaks all the rules.
Who is this Jesus? Looking closer, you realize
He's here to show how futile it is to trade God's
true righteousness for worthless rules made by
men. God's commands give life and promote
justice; man's rules crush the joy and love out of
everyone. Jesus is here to change all that, but not
without first bruising a few egos. This is, after all,
a revolution.*

Afterward Jesus returned to Jerusalem for one of the
Jewish holy days. Inside the city, near the Sheep
Gate, was the pool of Bethesda, with five covered
porches. Crowds of sick people—blind, lame, or
paralyzed—lay on the porches. One of the men lying
there had been sick for thirty-eight years. When
Jesus saw him and knew he had been ill for a long
time, he asked him, "Would you like to get well?"

"I can't, sir," the sick man said, "for I have no
one to put me into the pool when the water bubbles
up. Someone else always gets there ahead of me."

Jesus told him, "Stand up, pick up your mat,
and walk!"

Instantly, the man was healed! He rolled up his
sleeping mat and began walking! But this miracle
happened on the Sabbath, so the Jewish leaders
objected. They said to the man who was cured,

"You can't work on the Sabbath! The law doesn't allow you to carry that sleeping mat!"

But he replied, "The man who healed me told me, 'Pick up your mat and walk.' "

"Who said such a thing as that?" they demanded.

Jesus couldn't have been more provocative by healing on this sacred day. Don't misunderstand, Jesus keeps the Sabbath by resting from work as the command was originally intended and teaches others to keep it as well. However, the practice of the day is in serious need of an overhaul. What is going on?

Sabbath Controversy

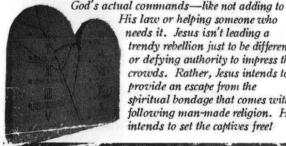

The Scribes have recorded the oral traditions of the Pharisees in a document called the Halakah (preserved in the Mishnah) which adds so much minutia to God's law that it destroyed the original purpose. For example, in order to make sure work is avoided, the oral law adds that one couldn't carry the following items on the Sabbath: paper, horse hairs, wax, a piece of broken earthenware, animal food, or anything that weighed more than three acorns (unless it was sewn into their clothes). Also, it was forbidden to eat food that had been prepared on the Sabbath. Most curious is the rule that one couldn't ever eat an egg if it was laid on the Sabbath! Maybe these seem silly, but why couldn't Jesus just compromise? Because Jesus knows that by keeping these man-made rules, He is guilty of breaking God's actual commands—like not adding to His law or helping someone who needs it. Jesus isn't leading a trendy rebellion just to be different or defying authority to impress the crowds. Rather, Jesus intends to provide an escape from the spiritual bondage that comes with following man-made religion. He intends to set the captives free!

The man didn't know, for Jesus had disappeared into the crowd. But afterward Jesus found him in the Temple and told him, "Now you are well; so stop sinning, or something even worse may happen to you." Then the man went and told the Jewish leaders that it was Jesus who had healed him.

So the Jewish leaders began harassing Jesus for breaking the Sabbath rules. But Jesus replied, "My Father is always working, and so am I." So the Jewish leaders tried all the harder to find a way to kill him. For he not only broke the Sabbath, he called God his Father, thereby making himself equal with God.

So Jesus explained, "I tell you the truth, the Son can do nothing by himself. He does only what he sees the Father doing. Whatever the Father does, the Son also does. For the Father loves the Son and shows him everything he is doing. In fact, the Father will show him how to do even greater works than healing this man. Then you will truly be astonished. For just as the Father gives life to those he raises from the dead, so the Son gives life to anyone he wants. In addition, the Father judges no one. Instead, he has given the Son absolute authority to judge, so that everyone will honor the Son, just as they honor the Father. Anyone who does not honor the Son is certainly not honoring the Father who sent him.

"I tell you the truth, those who listen to my message and believe in God who sent me have eternal life. They will never be condemned for their sins, but they have already passed from death into life.

"And I assure you that the time is coming, indeed it's here now, when the dead will hear my voice—the voice of the Son of God. And those who listen will live. The Father has life in himself, and he has granted that same life-giving power to his Son. And he has given him authority to judge everyone because he is the Son of Man. Don't be so surprised! Indeed, the time is coming when all the dead in their graves will hear the voice of God's Son, and they will rise again. Those who have done good will rise to experience eternal life, and those who have continued in evil will rise to experience judgment. I can do nothing on my own. I judge as God tells me. Therefore, my judgment is just, because I carry out the will of the one who sent me, not my own will.

"If I were to testify on my own behalf, my testimony would not be valid. But someone else is also testifying about me, and I assure you that everything he says about me is true. In fact, you sent investigators to listen to John the Baptist, and his testimony about me was true. Of course, I have no need of human witnesses, but I say these things so you might be saved. John was like a burning and shining lamp, and you were excited for a while about his message. But I have a greater witness than John—my teachings and my miracles. The Father gave me these works to accomplish, and they prove that he sent me. And the Father who sent me has testified about me himself. You have never heard his voice or seen him face to face, and you do not have his message in your hearts, because you do not believe me—the one he sent to you.

"You search the Scriptures because you think they give you eternal life. But the Scriptures point to me! Yet you refuse to come to me to receive this life.

"Your approval means nothing to me, because I know you don't have God's love within you. For I have come to you in my Father's name, and you have rejected me. Yet if others come in their own name, you gladly welcome them. No wonder you can't believe! For you gladly honor each other, but you don't care about the honor that comes from the one who alone is God.

"Yet it isn't I who will accuse you before the Father. Moses will accuse you! Yes, Moses, in whom you put your hopes. If you really believed Moses, you would believe me, because he wrote about me. But since you don't believe what he wrote, how will you believe what I say?"

The religious leaders are livid! But instead of shrinking back, Jesus continues to speak boldly—not to incite an uprising as much as to teach through correction. That's why Jesus decides to use the Sabbath once again to confront their false beliefs.

One Sabbath day as Jesus was walking through some grainfields, his disciples broke off heads of grain, rubbed off the husks in their hands, and ate the grain. But some Pharisees said, "Why are you breaking the law by harvesting grain on the Sabbath?"

Jesus said to them, "Haven't you ever read in the Scriptures what David did when he and his companions were hungry? He went into the house

Reflection

How does Jesus respond to being challenged about breaking the Pharisees' and Sabbath rules?

Jesus is directed and motivated by his relationship with his Father. How is your understanding of God impacting you and your relationships?

of God (during the days when Abiathar[16] was high priest) and broke the law by eating the sacred loaves of bread that only the priests are allowed to eat. He also gave some to his companions."

And haven't you read in the law of Moses that the priests on duty in the Temple may work on the Sabbath? I tell you, there is one here who is even greater than the Temple! But you would not have condemned my innocent disciples if you knew the meaning of this Scripture: 'I want you to show mercy, not offer sacrifices.' "

Then Jesus said to them, "The Sabbath was made to meet the needs of people, and not people to meet the requirements of the Sabbath. So the Son of Man is Lord, even over the Sabbath!"

On another Sabbath day, a man with a deformed right hand was in the synagogue while Jesus was teaching. The teachers of religious law and the Pharisees watched Jesus closely. If he healed the man's hand, they planned to accuse him of working on the Sabbath.

But Jesus knew their thoughts. He said to the man with the deformed hand, "Come and stand in front of everyone." So the man came forward. Then he turned to his critics and asked, "Does the law permit good deeds on the Sabbath, or is it a day for doing evil? Is this a day to save life or to destroy it?" But they wouldn't answer him.

---

[16] **Abiathar:** Jesus is appealing to an authority they would relate to—King David and a high priest (1 Samuel 21). At the time this incident occurred with David, Abiathar's father Ahimelech was technically high priest, but Abiathar would take over soon and becomes one of Israel's greatest high priests.

He looked around at them angrily and was deeply saddened by their hard hearts. And he said, "If you had a sheep that fell into a well on the Sabbath, wouldn't you work to pull it out? Of course you would. And how much more valuable is a person than a sheep! Yes, the law permits a person to do good on the Sabbath."

Then he said to the man, "Hold out your hand." So the man held out his hand, and it was restored, just like the other one! At this, the Pharisees went away wild with rage and met with the supporters of Herod to plot how to kill Jesus.

But Jesus knew what they were planning. So he left that area and went out to the lake with his disciples, and a large crowd followed him. They came from all over Galilee, Judea, Jerusalem, Idumea, from east of the Jordan River, and even from as far north as Tyre and Sidon. The news about his miracles had spread far and wide, and vast numbers of people came to see him.

Jesus instructed his disciples to have a boat ready so the crowd would not crush him. He had healed many people that day, so all the sick people eagerly pushed forward to touch him. And whenever those possessed by evil spirits caught sight of him, the spirits would throw them to the ground in front of him shrieking, "You are the Son of God!" But Jesus sternly commanded the spirits not to reveal who he was.

This fulfilled the prophecy of Isaiah concerning him:

"Look at my Servant, whom I have chosen. He is my Beloved, who pleases me. I will put my Spirit upon him, and he

will proclaim justice to the nations. He
will not fight or shout or raise his voice in
public. He will not crush the weakest reed
or put out a flickering candle. Finally he
will cause justice to be victorious. And his
name will be the hope of all the world."

⚬⟷⟜

One day soon afterward Jesus went up on a
mountain to pray, and he prayed to God all night.
At daybreak he called together all of his disciples
and chose twelve of them to be apostles. They were
to accompany him, and he would send them out to
preach, giving them authority to cast out demons.

Here are their names: Simon (whom he named
Peter), James and John (the sons of Zebedee, but
Jesus nicknamed them "Sons of Thunder"), Andrew,
Philip, Bartholomew, Matthew, Thomas, James (son
of Alphaeus), Thaddaeus, Simon (the zealot), Judas
Iscariot (who later betrayed him).

*We read about Jesus calling His disciples in
Chapter Two. Now He makes it official.
Formally naming the twelve disciples is so
monumental that Jesus spends the night praying
over it. Now Jesus and His twelve are ready to get
to work. But first, He must do some heavy-duty
teaching. The subject matter is the oh-so-familiar
law. Jesus teaches the law with insight and
authority like never heard before. Just like Moses
descended from the mountain with the Ten
Commandments for his people, Jesus instructs
His people from the mountainside. What He
teaches is the heart of what it means to know and
to love God.*

Reflection

🧠 What do
you see Jesus
communica-
ting about
God's heart as
He addresses
perspectives of
Sabbath Law?

💗 What are
you challenged
to view differ-
rently as you
follow Jesus?

One day as he saw the crowds gathering, Jesus went up on the mountainside and sat down. His disciples gathered around him, and he began to teach them.

"God blesses those who are poor and realize their need for him, for the Kingdom of Heaven is theirs.

God blesses those who mourn, for they will be comforted.

God blesses those who are humble, for they will inherit the whole earth.

God blesses those who hunger and thirst for justice, for they will be satisfied.

God blesses those who are merciful, for they will be shown mercy.

God blesses those whose hearts are pure, for they will see God.

God blesses those who work for peace, for they will be called the children of God.

God blesses those who are persecuted for doing right, for the Kingdom of Heaven is theirs.

"God blesses you when people hate you and exclude you and mock you and persecute you and lie about you and say all sorts of evil things against you because you are my followers. Be happy about it! Be very glad! For a great reward awaits you in heaven. And remember, the ancient prophets were persecuted in the same way.

What sorrow awaits you who are rich, for you have your only happiness now.

What sorrow awaits you who are fat and prosperous now, for a time of awful hunger awaits you.

What sorrow awaits you who laugh now, for your laughing will turn to mourning and sorrow.

What sorrow awaits you who are praised by the crowds, for their ancestors also praised false prophets.

"You are the salt of the earth. But what good is salt if it has lost its flavor? Can you make it salty again? It will be thrown out and trampled underfoot as worthless.

"You are the light of the world—like a city on a hilltop that cannot be hidden. No one lights a lamp and then puts it under a basket. Instead, a lamp is placed on a stand, where it gives light to everyone in the house. In the same way, let your good deeds shine out for all to see, so that everyone will praise your heavenly Father.

"Don't misunderstand why I have come. I did not come to abolish the law of Moses or the writings of the prophets. No, I came to accomplish their purpose. I tell you the truth, until heaven and earth disappear, not even the smallest detail of God's law will disappear until its purpose is achieved. So if you ignore the least commandment and teach others to do the same, you will be called the least in the Kingdom of Heaven. But anyone who obeys God's laws and teaches them will be called great in the Kingdom of Heaven.

"But I warn you—unless your righteousness is better than the righteousness of the teachers of

religious law and the Pharisees, you will never enter
the Kingdom of Heaven!"

> *Many today are under the false impression that*
> *since Jesus came to forgive, we don't have to obey*
> *God's law. However, Jesus clearly says He's not*
> *here to abolish the law but to fulfill it. Not only*
> *that, but He will re-establish the true standard of*
> *righteous-ness for His followers. First, since we*
> *are all sinners, we become righteous only through*
> *placing our faith in Jesus. Just as important,*
> *however, is that Jesus is inviting us into God's*
> *Kingdom. In this Kingdom, we follow Jesus as our*
> *Master, not a distorted version of God's law. This*
> *means obedience is much more than conforming on*
> *the outside, as many religious leaders were doing*
> *and teaching others to do. For citizens in God's*
> *Kingdom, obedience overflows from the heart. To*
> *demonstrate what He means by this, Jesus will*
> *now revolutionize six of God's major laws,*
> *proclaiming before each one: "You have heard . .*
> *. BUT I SAY . . ."*

"You have heard that our ancestors were told,
'You must not murder. If you commit murder, you
are subject to judgment.' But I say, if you are even
angry with someone, you are subject to judgment! If
you call someone an idiot, you are in danger of being
brought before the court. And if you curse someone,
you are in danger of the fires of hell.

"So if you are presenting a sacrifice at the altar
in the Temple and you suddenly remember that
someone has something against you, leave your
sacrifice there at the altar. Go and be reconciled to
that person. Then come and offer your sacrifice to
God.

"When you are on the way to court with your adversary, settle your differences quickly. Otherwise, your accuser may hand you over to the judge, who will hand you over to an officer, and you will be thrown into prison. And if that happens, you surely won't be free again until you have paid the last penny.

"You have heard the commandment that says, 'You must not commit adultery.' But I say, anyone who even looks at a woman with lust has already committed adultery with her in his heart. So if your eye—even your good eye—causes you to lust, gouge it out and throw it away. It is better for you to lose one part of your body than for your whole body to be thrown into hell. And if your hand—even your stronger hand—causes you to sin, cut it off and throw it away. It is better for you to lose one part of your body than for your whole body to be thrown into hell.

"You have heard the law that says, 'A man can divorce his wife by merely giving her a written notice of divorce.' But I say that a man who divorces his wife, unless she has been unfaithful, causes her to commit adultery. And anyone who marries a divorced woman also commits adultery.

"You have also heard that our ancestors were told, 'You must not break your vows; you must carry out the vows you make to the LORD.' But I say, do not make any vows! Do not say, 'By heaven!' because heaven is God's throne. And do not say, 'By the earth!' because the earth is his footstool. And do not say, 'By Jerusalem!' for Jerusalem is the city of the great King. Do not even say, 'By my head!' for you can't turn one hair white or black. Just say a

Reflection

Jesus chooses twelve of the disciples who are following him. What do you notice about what he teaches them?

As you reflect on the things Jesus is teaching here, what would you ask him to do in your heart?

simple, 'Yes, I will,' or 'No, I won't.' Anything beyond this is from the evil one.

❧

"You have heard the law that says the punishment must match the injury: 'An eye for an eye, and a tooth for a tooth.' But I say, do not resist an evil person! If someone slaps you on the right cheek, offer the other cheek also. If you are sued in court and your shirt is taken from you, give your coat, too. If a soldier demands that you carry his gear for a mile, carry it two miles. Give to those who ask, and don't turn away from those who want to borrow.

"You have heard the law that says, 'Love your neighbor' and hate your enemy. But I say, love your enemies! Pray for those who persecute you! In that way, you will be acting as true children of your Father in heaven. For he gives his sunlight to both the evil and the good, and he sends rain on the just and the unjust alike. If you love only those who love you, what reward is there for that? Even corrupt tax collectors do that much. If you are kind only to your friends, how are you different from anyone else? Even pagans do that. But you are to be perfect, even as your Father in heaven is perfect."

> *These six commands were never meant to be a complete list but are to portray a citizen in God's Kingdom. Jesus ends with the command to be perfect like God is perfect. Perfect?! Who can live up to such a standard? It's important to know that the Greek word Jesus uses for "perfect" is* teleios, *which does not mean "without flaw," but means "mature, whole, complete." Therefore, Jesus*

is not saying that we need to be morally flawless like God is, but He is calling us to love maturely and completely like God does. Citizens of God's Kingdom are to reflect the character of the King, therefore we are to "love, because God is love." He will now finish this incredible teaching, covering a variety of topics all pointing to truly righteous living.

"Watch out! Don't do your good deeds publicly, to be admired by others, for you will lose the reward from your Father in heaven. When you give to someone in need, don't do as the hypocrites do—blowing trumpets in the synagogues and streets to call attention to their acts of charity! I tell you the truth, they have received all the reward they will ever get. But when you give to someone in need, don't let your left hand know what your right hand is doing. Give your gifts in private, and your Father, who sees everything, will reward you.

"When you pray, don't be like the hypocrites who love to pray publicly on street corners and in the synagogues where everyone can see them. I tell you the truth, that is all the reward they will ever get. But when you pray, go away by yourself, shut the door behind you, and pray to your Father in private. Then your Father, who sees everything, will reward you.

Reflection

Which of Jesus's teachings here surprises you or stands out to you? Why?

Where do you struggle with wanting people to see and respect your good deeds?

"When you pray, don't babble on and on as people of other religions do. They think their prayers are answered merely by repeating their words again and again. Don't be like them, for your Father

knows exactly what you need even before you ask
him! Pray like this:

> Our Father in heaven, may your name be
> kept holy.

> May your Kingdom come soon. May your
> will be done on earth, as it is in heaven.

> Give us today the food we need, and
> forgive us our sins, as we have forgiven
> those who sin against us.

> And don't let us yield to temptation, but
> rescue us from the evil one. "If you
> forgive those who sin against you, your
> heavenly Father will forgive you. But if
> you refuse to forgive others, your Father
> will not forgive your sins.

"And when you fast, don't make it obvious, as
the hypocrites do, for they try to look miserable and
disheveled so people will admire them for their
fasting. I tell you the truth, that is the only reward
they will ever get. But when you fast, comb your hair
and wash your face. Then no one will notice that
you are fasting, except your Father, who knows what
you do in private. And your Father, who sees
everything, will reward you.

"Don't store up treasures here on earth, where
moths eat them and rust destroys them, and where
thieves break in and steal. Store your treasures in
heaven, where moths and rust cannot destroy, and
thieves do not break in and steal. Wherever your
treasure is, there the desires of your heart will also
be.

"Your eye is a lamp that provides light for your
body. When your eye is good, your whole body is

filled with light. But when your eye is bad, your whole body is filled with darkness. And if the light you think you have is actually darkness, how deep that darkness is!

"No one can serve two masters. For you will hate one and love the other; you will be devoted to one and despise the other. You cannot serve both God and money.

"That is why I tell you not to worry about everyday life—whether you have enough food and drink, or enough clothes to wear. Isn't life more than food, and your body more than clothing? Look at the birds. They don't plant or harvest or store food in barns, for your heavenly Father feeds them. And aren't you far more valuable to him than they are? Can all your worries add a single moment to your life?

"And why worry about your clothing? Look at the lilies of the field and how they grow. They don't work or make their clothing, yet Solomon in all his glory was not dressed as beautifully as they are. And if God cares so wonderfully for wildflowers that are here today and thrown into the fire tomorrow, he will certainly care for you. Why do you have so little faith?

"So don't worry about these things, saying, 'What will we eat? What will we drink? What will we wear?' These things dominate the thoughts of unbelievers, but your heavenly Father already knows all your needs. Seek the Kingdom of God above all else, and live righteously, and he will give you everything you need.

"So don't worry about tomorrow, for tomorrow will bring its own worries. Today's trouble is enough for today.

"Do not judge others, and you will not be judged. Do not condemn others, or it will all come back against you. Forgive others, and you will be forgiven. Give, and you will receive. Your gift will return to you in full—pressed down, shaken together to make room for more, running over, and poured into your lap. The amount you give will determine the amount you get back. For you will be treated as you treat others. The standard you use in judging is the standard by which you will be judged.

"And why worry about a speck in your friend's eye when you have a log in your own? How can you think of saying to your friend, 'Let me help you get rid of that speck in your eye,' when you can't see past the log in your own eye? Hypocrite! First get rid of the log in your own eye; then you will see well enough to deal with the speck in your friend's eye.

"Don't waste what is holy on people who are unholy. Don't throw your pearls to pigs! They will trample the pearls, then turn and attack you.

"Keep on asking, and you will receive what you ask for. Keep on seeking, and you will find. Keep on knocking, and the door will be opened to you. For everyone who asks, receives. Everyone who seeks, finds. And to everyone who knocks, the door will be opened.

"You parents—if your children ask for a loaf of bread, do you give them a stone instead? Or if they ask for a fish, do you give them a snake? Of course not! So if you sinful people know how to give good gifts to your children, how much more will your heavenly Father give good gifts to those who ask him.

"Do to others whatever you would like them to do to you. This is the essence of all that is taught in the law and the prophets.

"You can enter God's Kingdom only through the narrow gate. The highway to hell is broad, and its gate is wide for the many who choose that way. But the gateway to life is very narrow and the road is difficult, and only a few ever find it.

"Beware of false prophets who come disguised as harmless sheep but are really vicious wolves. You can identify them by their fruit, that is, by the way they act. Can you pick grapes from thornbushes, or figs from thistles? A good tree produces good fruit, and a bad tree produces bad fruit. A good tree can't produce bad fruit, and a bad tree can't produce good fruit. So every tree that does not produce good fruit is chopped down and thrown into the fire. Yes, just as you can identify a tree by its fruit, so you can identify people by their actions.

"A good person produces good things from the treasury of a good heart, and an evil person produces evil things from the treasury of an evil heart. What you say flows from what is in your heart.

"Not everyone who calls out to me, 'Lord! Lord!' will enter the Kingdom of Heaven. Only those who actually do the will of my Father in heaven will enter. On judgment day many will say to me, 'Lord! Lord! We prophesied in your name and cast out demons in your name and performed many miracles in your name.' But I will reply, 'I never knew you. Get away from me, you who break God's laws.'

"Anyone who listens to my teaching and follows it is wise, like a person who builds a house on solid rock. Though the rain comes in torrents and the floodwaters rise and the winds beat against that house, it won't collapse because it is built on bedrock. But anyone who hears my teaching and ignores it is foolish, like a person who builds a house on sand. When the rains and floods come and the winds beat against that house, it will collapse with a mighty crash."

When Jesus had finished saying these things, the crowds were amazed at his teaching, for he taught with real authority—quite unlike their teachers of religious law. Large crowds followed Jesus as he came down the mountainside.

Reflection

🖤 As Jesus teaches what does he say about a person's heart?

🖤 What do you notice 'flowing from your heart' as you speak?

Lest anyone walk away from Jesus' words thinking, "Boy that was entertaining, those are great ideas," Jesus ends it with a stern warning about wise and foolish people. Foolish people are those that ignore His words and are ultimately destroyed in judgment. Wise people are those that hear and practice what Jesus taught.

❧

Scripture References

John 5; Matthew 12:1–21; 5:1—7:29; 8:1; Mark 2:23—3:19; Luke 6:1–26; 14:35; Acts 1:13

Chapter 5

Crowds Grow as Jesus Reveals Power

After Jesus' great sermon He returns to Capernaum. Word about Him has spread, and Jesus' fame is growing. His reputation will only intensify from here as He displays even more of His power through a significant number of miraculous acts.

When Jesus had finished saying all this to the people, he returned to Capernaum. At that time the highly valued slave of a Roman officer was paralyzed, in terrible pain, and near death. When the officer heard about Jesus, he sent some respected Jewish elders to ask him to come and heal his slave. So they earnestly begged Jesus to help the man. "If anyone deserves your help, he does," they said, "for he loves the Jewish people and even built a synagogue for us."

So Jesus went with them. But just before they arrived at the house, the officer sent some friends to say, "Lord, don't trouble yourself by coming to my home, for I am not worthy of such an honor. I am not even worthy to come and meet you. Just say the word from where you are, and my servant will be healed. I know this because I am under the authority of my superior officers, and I have authority over my soldiers. I only need to say, 'Go,' and they go, or 'Come,' and they come. And if I say to my slaves, 'Do this,' they do it."

When Jesus heard this, he was amazed. Turning to those who were following him, he said, "I tell you the truth, I haven't seen faith like this in all Israel! And I tell you this, that many Gentiles will come

from all over the world—from east and west—and
sit down with Abraham, Isaac, and Jacob at the feast
in the Kingdom of Heaven. But many Israelites—
those for whom the Kingdom was prepared—will
be thrown into outer darkness, where there will be
weeping and gnashing of teeth."

Then Jesus said to the Roman officer, "Go back
home. Because you believed, it has happened." And
the young servant was healed that same hour. When
the officer's friends returned to his house, they
found the slave completely healed.

Soon afterward Jesus went with his disciples to
the village of Nain, and a large crowd followed him.
A funeral procession was coming out as he
approached the village gate. The young man who
had died was a widow's only son, and a large crowd
from the village was with her. When the Lord saw
her, his heart overflowed with compassion. "Don't
cry!" he said. Then he walked over to the coffin and
touched it, and the bearers stopped. "Young man,"
he said, "I tell you, get up." Then the dead boy sat
up and began to talk! And Jesus gave him back to his
mother.

Great fear swept the crowd, and they praised
God, saying, "A mighty prophet has risen among
us," and "God has visited his people today." And
the news about Jesus spread throughout Judea and
the surrounding countryside.

The disciples of John the Baptist, who was in
prison, told John about everything Jesus was doing.
So John called for two of his disciples, and he sent
them to the Lord to ask him, "Are you the Messiah
we've been expecting, or should we keep looking for
someone else?"

John's two disciples found Jesus and said to him, "John the Baptist sent us to ask, 'Are you the Messiah we've been expecting, or should we keep looking for someone else?' "

At that very time, Jesus cured many people of their diseases and illnesses, and he cast out evil spirits and restored sight to many who were blind. Then he told John's disciples, "Go back to John and tell him what you have seen and heard—the blind see, the lame walk, the lepers are cured, the deaf hear, the dead are raised to life, and the Good News is being preached to the poor. And tell him, 'God blesses those who do not turn away because of me.' "

After John's disciples left, Jesus began talking about him to the crowds. "What kind of man did you go into the wilderness to see? Was he a weak reed, swayed by every breath of wind? Or were you expecting to see a man dressed in expensive clothes? No, people who wear beautiful clothes and live in luxury are found in palaces. Were you looking for a prophet? Yes, and he is more than a prophet. John is the man to whom the Scriptures refer when they say,

'Look, I am sending my messenger ahead
of you, and he will prepare your way
before you.'

"I tell you, of all who have ever lived, none is greater than John the Baptist. Yet even the least person in the Kingdom of God is greater than he is!" And from the time John the Baptist began preaching until now, the Kingdom of Heaven has been forcefully advancing, and violent people are attacking it. For before John came, all the prophets and the law of Moses looked forward to this present time. And if you are willing to accept what I say, he is Elijah, the one the prophets said would come. Anyone with ears to hear should listen and understand!"

When they heard this, all the people—even the tax collectors—agreed that God's way was right, for they had been baptized by John. But the Pharisees and experts in religious law rejected God's plan for them, for they had refused John's baptism.

"To what can I compare the people of this generation?" Jesus asked. "How can I describe them? They are like children playing a game in the public square. They complain to their friends,

'We played wedding songs, and you didn't dance, so we played funeral songs, and you didn't weep.'[17]

For John the Baptist didn't spend his time eating bread or drinking wine, and you say, 'He's possessed by a demon.' The Son of Man, on the other hand, feasts and drinks, and you say, 'He's a glutton and a drunkard, and a friend of tax collectors and other sinners!' But wisdom is shown to be right by the lives of those who follow it."

Then Jesus began to denounce the towns where he had done so many of his miracles, because they

---

[17] **didn't dance . . . didn't weep**: Jesus is evaluating this culture as malcontent. They'll neither dance for a happy occasion nor will they weep when there's sadness. What's this mean? On the one hand, they don't celebrate Jesus' grace but call him "friend of sinners" because he embraces sinners instead of condemning them. On the other hand, they don't like John the Baptist because of his strict moral code and message of radical repentance.

hadn't repented of their sins and turned to God. "What sorrow awaits you, Korazin and Bethsaida![18] For if the miracles I did in you had been done in wicked Tyre and Sidon, their people would have repented of their sins long ago, clothing themselves in burlap and throwing ashes on their heads to show their remorse. I tell you, Tyre and Sidon will be better off on judgment day than you.

"And you people of Capernaum, will you be honored in heaven? No, you will go down to the place of the dead. For if the miracles I did for you had been done in wicked Sodom, it would still be here today. I tell you, even Sodom will be better off on judgment day than you."

At that time Jesus prayed this prayer: "O Father, Lord of heaven and earth, thank you for hiding these things from those who think themselves wise and clever, and for revealing them to the childlike. Yes, Father, it pleased you to do it this way!

"My Father has entrusted everything to me. No one truly knows the Son except the Father, and no one truly knows the Father except the Son and those to whom the Son chooses to reveal him."

Then Jesus said, "Come to me, all of you who are weary and carry heavy burdens, and I will give

---

[18] **Korazin and Bethsaida:** Korazin and Bethsaida were suburbs of Capernaum, which was where Jesus performed many miracles and works of compassion. Although the crowds enjoyed Jesus, they did not respond in repentance. Therefore, Jesus compares them to two cities that represented the epitome of Israel's enemies—Tyre and Sidon (Isaiah 23; Ezekiel 26–38; Amos 1:9–10) plus Sodom (Genesis 19).

you rest. Take my yoke[19] upon you. Let me teach
you, because I am humble and gentle at heart, and
you will find rest for your souls. For my yoke is easy
to bear, and the burden I give you is light."

*Even after Jesus is rejected by people who witness
miracle after miracle, He is still gracious. He
follows these rejections with an offer for eternal
life. The yoke of Judaism of that day was crushing
under the demands of the law. Jesus offers them a
new yoke—the yoke of partnership with Him,
where He does the heavy-lifting! Next we will see
just how freeing it is to have the burden of sin
lifted and just how refreshing it is to follow Jesus.*

Reflection

What amazes Jesus about the Roman officer?

Has there ever been a time when you didn't want to bather Jesus with your request / problem / need?

One of the Pharisees asked Jesus to have dinner
with him, so Jesus went to his home and sat down to
eat. When a certain immoral woman from that city
heard he was eating there, she brought a beautiful
alabaster jar filled with expensive perfume. Then she
knelt behind him at his feet, weeping. Her tears fell
on his feet, and she wiped them off with her hair.
Then she kept kissing his feet and putting perfume
on them.

When the Pharisee who had invited him saw
this, he said to himself, "If this man were a prophet,

---

[19] **yoke**: The yoke of Jesus' day was a fitted collar-like
frame, shaped to rest on the neck and shoulders of two
animals. Teamed together, the task was far easier for two
oxen than for one. And if one were a young ox, how much
easier to have an older, stronger companion to share the
burden. To those who called for God's King to reign over
them, Jesus offered to be God's Servant, yoked in harness
with them.

he would know what kind of woman is touching him. She's a sinner!"

Then Jesus answered his thoughts. "Simon," he said to the Pharisee, "I have something to say to you."

"Go ahead, Teacher," Simon replied.

Then Jesus told him this story: "A man loaned money to two people—500 pieces of silver to one and 50 pieces to the other. But neither of them could repay him, so he kindly forgave them both, canceling their debts. Who do you suppose loved him more after that?"

Simon answered, "I suppose the one for whom he canceled the larger debt."

"That's right," Jesus said. Then he turned to the woman and said to Simon, "Look at this woman kneeling here. When I entered your home, you didn't offer me water to wash the dust from my feet, but she has washed them with her tears and wiped them with her hair. You didn't greet me with a kiss, but from the time I first came in, she has not stopped kissing my feet. You neglected the courtesy of olive oil to anoint my head, but she has anointed my feet with rare perfume.

"I tell you, her sins—and they are many—have been forgiven, so she has shown me much love. But a person who is forgiven little shows only little love." Then Jesus said to the woman, "Your sins are for-given."

The men at the table said among themselves, "Who is this man, that he goes around forgiving sins?"

And Jesus said to the woman, "Your faith has saved you; go in peace."

Soon afterward Jesus began a tour of the nearby towns and villages, preaching and announcing the Good News about the Kingdom of God. He took his twelve disciples with him, along with some women who had been cured of evil spirits and diseases. Among them were Mary Magdalene, from whom he had cast out seven demons; Joanna, the wife of Chuza, Herod's business manager; Susanna; and many others who were contributing from their own resources to support Jesus and his disciples.

One time Jesus entered a house, and the crowds began to gather again. Soon he and his disciples couldn't even find time to eat. When his family heard what was happening, they tried to take him away. "He's out of his mind," they said.

Then a demon-possessed man, who was blind and couldn't speak, was brought to Jesus. He healed the man so that he could both speak and see. The crowd was amazed and asked, "Could it be that Jesus is the Son of David, the Messiah?"

But when the Pharisees heard about the miracle, they said, "No wonder he can cast out demons. He gets his power from Satan, the prince of demons."

Jesus knew their thoughts and replied, "Any kingdom divided by civil war is doomed. A town or family splintered by feuding will fall apart. And if Satan is casting out Satan, he is divided and fighting against himself. His own kingdom will not survive. And if I am empowered by Satan, what about your own exorcists? They cast out demons, too, so they will condemn you for what you have said. But if I am casting out demons by the Spirit of God, then the Kingdom of God has arrived among you. For who is powerful enough to enter the house of a strong man like Satan and plunder his goods? Only someone even stronger—someone who could tie him up and then plunder his house.

"Anyone who isn't with me opposes me, and anyone who isn't working with me is actually working against me.

"So I tell you, every sin and blasphemy can be forgiven—except blasphemy against the Holy Spirit,[20] which will never be forgiven. Anyone who speaks against the Son of Man can be forgiven, but anyone who speaks against the Holy Spirit will never be forgiven, either in this world or in the world to come." He told them this because they were saying, "He's possessed by an evil spirit."

"A tree is identified by its fruit. If a tree is good, its fruit will be good. If a tree is bad, its fruit will be bad. You brood of snakes! How could evil men like you speak what is good and right? For whatever is in your heart determines what you say. A good person produces good things from the treasury of a good heart, and an evil person produces evil things from the treasury of an evil heart. And I tell you this, you must give an account on judgment day for every idle word you speak. The words you say will either acquit you or condemn you."

One day some teachers of religious law and Pharisees came to Jesus and said, "Teacher, we want

---

[20] **blasphemy against the Holy Spirit**: Blasphemy against the Spirit of God means that a person has willfully refused to believe in the work of God. Thus, by definition, God cannot grant forgiveness to a person who has no faith in Him. If someone wonders whether they have committed this sin or not, the fact that they are concerned seems to exclude the possibility of their having done it. Willful rejection of God's purpose is the problem, not a single word or deed.

you to show us a miraculous sign to prove your authority."

As the crowd pressed in on Jesus, he said, "Only an evil, adulterous generation would demand a miraculous sign; but the only sign I will give them is the sign of the prophet Jonah. For as Jonah was in the belly of the great fish for three days and three nights, so will the Son of Man be in the heart of the earth for three days and three nights.

"The people of Nineveh[21] will stand up against this generation on judgment day and condemn it, for they repented of their sins at the preaching of Jonah. Now someone greater than Jonah is here—but you refuse to repent. The queen of Sheba will also stand up against this generation on judgment day and condemn it, for she came from a distant land to hear the wisdom of Solomon. Now someone greater than Solomon is here—but you refuse to listen.

"When an evil spirit leaves a person, it goes into the desert, seeking rest but finding none. Then it says, 'I will return to the person I came from.' So it returns and finds its former home empty, swept, and in order. Then the spirit finds seven other spirits more evil than itself, and they all enter the person and live there. And so that person is worse off than before. That will be the experience of this evil generation."

These skeptics are seeking, but not wanting to find. Jesus has given them plenty of signs.

---

[21] **people of Nineveh**: The book of Jonah in the Old Testament tells about how the people of Nineveh were going to be destroyed because of their sin unless they repented. God sent His prophet Jonah to warn them first and they were ultimately spared after heeding Jonah's warning. To be compared to Nineveh was a serious indictment from Jesus.

However, a sign will come that will trump everything—the sign of Jonah. No, Jesus won't spend any time in the belly of a fish. Rather, He will be resurrected after spending time in the heart of the earth following His crucifixion. Jesus knows that this generation is in dangerous territory. To reject God's Messiah is to invite Satan to have his way. So Jesus will continue to teach, hoping they will one day understand. He will now turn to parables to present His message. As usual, His message will be confusing to some while dazzling to others.

As Jesus was speaking to the crowd, his mother and brothers came to see him, but they couldn't get to him because of the crowd. They sent word for him to come out and talk with them. Someone told Jesus, "Your mother and your brothers are outside, and they want to speak to you."

Jesus asked, "Who is my mother? Who are my brothers?" Then he looked at those around him and said, "Look, these are my mother and brothers. My mother and my brothers are all those who hear God's word and obey it."

Reflection

🖐 How does Jesus respond to Simon? The woman?

💜 How can you show Jesus honor daily? How do you nurture gratitude in your life?

Later that same day Jesus left the house and sat beside the lake. A large crowd from many towns soon gathered around him, so he got into a boat. Then he sat there and taught as the people stood on the shore. He told many stories in the form of parables, such as this one:

"Listen! A farmer went out to plant some seeds. As he scattered them across his field, some seeds fell on a footpath, where they were stepped on, and the birds came and ate them. Other seeds fell on shallow soil with underlying rock. The seeds sprouted quickly because the soil was shallow. But the plants soon wilted under the hot sun, and since they didn't have deep roots, they died. Other seeds fell among thorns that grew up with them and choked out the tender plants. Still other seeds fell on fertile soil, and they produced a crop that was thirty, sixty, and even a hundred times as much as had been planted!" When he had said this, he called out, "Anyone with ears to hear should listen and understand."

His disciples came and asked him, "Why do you use parables when you talk to the people?"

He replied, "You are permitted to understand the secrets of the Kingdom of Heaven, but others are not. I use parables for everything I say to outsiders. To those who listen to my teaching, more understanding will be given, and they will have an abundance of knowledge. But for those who are not listening, even what little understanding they have will be taken away from them. That is why I use these parables,

> For they look, but they don't really see.
> They hear, but they don't really listen or understand.

This fulfills the prophecy of Isaiah that says,

> 'When you hear what I say, you will not understand. When you see what I do, you will not comprehend. For the hearts of these people are hardened, and their ears cannot hear, and they have closed their eyes—so their eyes cannot see, and their ears cannot hear, and their hearts cannot

understand, and they cannot turn to me and let me heal them.'

"But blessed are your eyes, because they see; and your ears, because they hear. I tell you the truth, many prophets and righteous people longed to see what you see, but they didn't see it. And they longed to hear what you hear, but they didn't hear it.

Then Jesus said to them, "If you can't understand the meaning of this parable, how will you understand all the other parables?

"Now listen to the explanation of the parable about the farmer planting seeds: The seed that fell on the footpath represents those who hear the message about the Kingdom and don't understand it. Then the evil one comes and snatches away the seed that was planted in their hearts and prevents them from believing and being saved. The seed on the rocky soil represents those who hear the message and immediately receive it with joy. But since they don't have deep roots, they don't last long. They fall away as soon as they have temptations, problems, or are persecuted for believing God's word. The seed that fell among the thorns represents those who hear God's word, but all too quickly the message is crowded out by the worries and pleasures of this life and the lure of wealth, so no fruit is produced. The seed that fell on good soil represents those who truly hear and accept God's word, cling to it, and patiently produce a harvest of thirty, sixty, or even a hundred times as much as had been planted!"

Then Jesus asked them, "Would anyone light a lamp and then put it under a basket or under a bed? Of course not! A lamp is placed on a stand, where its light can be seen by all who enter the house. For all that is secret will eventually be brought into the open, and everything that is concealed will be brought to light and made known to all. Anyone with ears to hear should listen and understand.

"So pay attention to how you hear. To those who listen to my teaching, more understanding will be given. But for those who are not listening, even what they think they understand will be taken away from them."

Jesus also said, "The Kingdom of God is like a farmer who scatters seed on the ground. Night and day, while he's asleep or awake, the seed sprouts and grows, but he does not understand how it happens. The earth produces the crops on its own. First a leaf blade pushes through, then the heads of wheat are formed, and finally the grain ripens. And as soon as the grain is ready, the farmer comes and harvests it with a sickle, for the harvest time has come."

Here is another story Jesus told: "The Kingdom of Heaven is like a farmer who planted good seed in his field. But that night as the workers slept, his enemy came and planted weeds among the wheat, then slipped away. When the crop began to grow and produce grain, the weeds also grew.

"The farmer's workers went to him and said, 'Sir, the field where you planted that good seed is full of weeds! Where did they come from?'

" 'An enemy has done this!' the farmer exclaimed.

" 'Should we pull out the weeds?' they asked.

" 'No,' he replied, 'you'll uproot the wheat if you do. Let both grow together until the harvest. Then I will tell the harvesters to sort out the weeds, tie them into bundles, and burn them, and to put the wheat in the barn.' "

Jesus said, "How can I describe the Kingdom of God? What story should I use to illustrate it? It is like a mustard seed planted in the ground. It is the smallest of all seeds, but it becomes the largest of all garden plants; it grows long branches, and birds can make nests in its shade."

Jesus also used this illustration: "The Kingdom of Heaven is like the yeast a woman used in making bread. Even though she put only a little yeast in three measures of flour, it permeated every part of the dough."

Jesus used many similar stories and illustrations to teach the people as much as they could understand. In fact, in his public ministry he never taught without using parables; but afterward, when he was alone with his disciples, he explained everything to them. This fulfilled what God had spoken through the prophet:

"I will speak to you in parables. I will explain things hidden since the creation of the world."

Then, leaving the crowds outside, Jesus went into the house. His disciples said, "Please explain to us the story of the weeds in the field."

Jesus replied, "The Son of Man is the farmer who plants the good seed. The field is the world, and the good seed represents the people of the Kingdom. The weeds are the people who belong to the evil one. The enemy who planted the weeds among the wheat is the devil. The harvest is the end of the world, and the harvesters are the angels.

"Just as the weeds are sorted out and burned in the fire, so it will be at the end of the world. The Son of Man will send his angels, and they will remove from his Kingdom everything that causes sin and all who do evil. And the angels will throw them into the fiery furnace, where there will be weeping and gnashing of teeth. Then the righteous will shine like the sun in their Father's Kingdom. Anyone with ears to hear should listen and understand!

"The Kingdom of Heaven is like a treasure that a man discovered hidden in a field. In his excitement, he hid it again and sold everything he owned to get enough money to buy the field.

"Again, the Kingdom of Heaven is like a merchant on the lookout for choice pearls. When he discovered a pearl of great value, he sold everything he owned and bought it!

"Again, the Kingdom of Heaven is like a fishing net that was thrown into the water and caught fish of every kind. When the net was full, they dragged it up onto the shore, sat down, and sorted the good fish into crates, but threw the bad ones away. That is the way it will be at the end of the world. The angels will come and separate the wicked people from the righteous, throwing the wicked into the fiery furnace, where there will be weeping and gnashing of teeth. Do you understand all these things?"

"Yes," they said, "we do."

Then he added, "Every teacher of religious law who becomes a disciple in the Kingdom of Heaven is like a homeowner who brings from his storeroom new gems of truth as well as old."

When Jesus had finished telling these stories and illustrations, he left that part of the country.

Reflection

 What war-
nings   does
Jesus give in
his parables?

Which of
the soils have
you experien-
ced in your
life?

*Once Jesus finishes His parables, the crowd
lingers, wanting to hear more. Jesus knows if He
and His disciples don't get away now, there will
be no time for rest. So they break away, but not
without some boats following along. As the wind
beats against the side of the boats, the waves
white-cap and the storm moves in; anyone on the
water will soon discover that the lake is the last
place they want to be…*

As evening came, when Jesus saw the crowd
around him, he said to his disciples, "Let's cross to
the other side of the lake." So they took Jesus in the
boat and started out, leaving the crowds behind
(although other boats followed). But suddenly a
fierce storm came up. High waves were breaking
into the boat, and it began to fill with water, and
they were in real danger.

Jesus was sleeping at the back of the boat with
his head on a cushion. The disciples woke him up,
shouting, "Teacher, don't you care that we're going
to drown?"

When Jesus woke up, he rebuked the wind and
said to the water, "Silence! Be still!" Suddenly the
wind stopped, and there was a great calm. Then he
asked them, "Why are you afraid? Do you still have
no faith?"

The disciples were absolutely terrified. "Who is
this man?" they asked each other. "Even the wind
and waves obey him!"

So they arrived at the other side of the lake, in
the region of the Gerasenes, across the lake from

Galilee. When Jesus climbed out of the boat, a man[22] possessed by an evil spirit came out from a cemetery to meet him. This man lived among the burial caves and could no longer be restrained, even with a chain. Even when he was placed under guard and put into chains and shackles—as he often was—he snapped the chains from his wrists and smashed the shackles. No one was strong enough to subdue him. Day and night he wandered among the burial caves and in the hills, howling and cutting himself with sharp stones and no one could go through that area.

When Jesus was still some distance away, the man saw him, ran to meet him, and bowed low before him. With a shriek, he screamed, "Why are you interfering with me, Jesus, Son of the Most High God? In the name of God, I beg you, don't torture me!" For Jesus had already said to the spirit, "Come out of the man, you evil spirit."

Then Jesus demanded, "What is your name?"

And he replied, "My name is Legion, because there are many of us inside this man." Then the evil spirits begged him again and again not to send them to some distant place.

There happened to be a large herd of pigs feeding on the hillside nearby. "If you cast us out, send us into those pigs," the spirits begged. "Let us enter them."

So Jesus gave them permission. The evil spirits came out of the man and entered the pigs, and the entire herd of 2,000 pigs plunged down the steep hillside into the lake and drowned in the water.

---

[22] **a man**: Matthew tells us there are two demon-possessed men. Mark and Luke only concentrate on the one who did the speaking, the more prominent of the two.

The herdsmen fled to the nearby town and the surrounding countryside, spreading the news as they ran. People rushed out to see what had happened. A crowd soon gathered around Jesus, and they saw the man who had been possessed by the legion of demons. He was sitting at Jesus' feet, fully clothed and perfectly sane, and they were all afraid. Then those who had seen what happened told the others about the demon-possessed man and the pigs. And the crowd began pleading with Jesus to go away and leave them alone, for a great wave of fear swept over them.

As Jesus was getting into the boat, the man who had been demon possessed begged to go with him. But Jesus said, "No, go home to your family, and tell them everything the Lord has done for you and how merciful he has been." So the man started off to visit the Ten Towns of that region and began to proclaim the great things Jesus had done for him; and everyone was amazed at what he told them.

Reflection

How does Jesus respond in a crisis or a potentially stressful situation?

If you were a disciple with Jesus at this time, what would be going through your mind as you watched all that Jesus did?

Jesus got into the boat again and went back to the other side of the lake, where a large crowd gathered around him on the shore, because they had been waiting for him. Then a leader of the local synagogue, whose name was Jairus, arrived. When he saw Jesus, he fell at his feet, pleading fervently with him to come home with him. "My little daughter is dying," he said. "Please come and lay your hands on her; heal her so she can live."

Jesus went with him, and all the people followed, crowding around him. A woman in the crowd had suffered for twelve years with constant bleeding. She had suffered a great deal from many doctors, and over the years she had spent everything she had to pay them, but she had gotten no better. In fact, she had gotten worse. She had heard about Jesus, so she came up behind him through the crowd and touched the fringe of his robe. For she thought to herself, "If I can just touch his robe, I will be healed." Immediately the bleeding stopped, and she could feel in her body that she had been healed of her terrible condition.

Jesus realized at once that healing power had gone out from him, so he turned around in the crowd and asked, "Who touched my robe?"

Everyone denied it, and Peter said, "Master, look at this crowd pressing around you. How can you ask, 'Who touched me?' "

But Jesus said, "Someone deliberately touched me, for I felt healing power go out from me."

Jesus kept on looking around to see who had done it. Then the frightened woman, trembling at the realization of what had happened to her, came and fell at his feet and the whole crowd heard her explain why she had touched him and that she had been im-mediately healed. And he said to her, "Daughter, your faith has made you well. Go in peace. Your suffering is over."

While he was still speaking to her, messengers arrived from the home of Jairus, the leader of the synagogue. They told him, "Your daughter is dead. There's no use troubling the Teacher now."

But Jesus overheard them and said to Jairus, "Don't be afraid. Just have faith, and she will be healed."

Then Jesus stopped the crowd and wouldn't let anyone go with him except Peter, James, and John (the brother of James), and the little girl's father and mother. When they came to the home of the synagogue leader, Jesus saw much commotion and weeping and wailing. He went inside and asked, "Why all this commotion and weeping? The child isn't dead; she's only asleep."

The crowd laughed at him because they all knew she had died. But he made them all leave, and he took the girl's father and mother and his three disciples into the room where the girl was lying. Holding her hand, he said to her, *"Talitha koum,"* which means "Little girl, get up!" And the girl, who was twelve years old, immediately stood up and walked around! They were overwhelmed and totally amazed. Jesus gave them strict orders not to tell anyone what had happened, and then he told them to give her something to eat. The report of this miracle swept through the entire countryside.

After Jesus left the girl's home, two blind men followed along behind him, shouting, "Son of David, have mercy on us!"

They went right into the house where he was staying, and Jesus asked them, "Do you believe I can make you see?"

"Yes, Lord," they told him, "we do."

Then he touched their eyes and said, "Because of your faith, it will happen." Then their eyes were opened, and they could see! Jesus sternly warned them, "Don't tell anyone about this." But instead, they went out and spread his fame all over the region.

When they left, a demon-possessed man who couldn't speak was brought to Jesus. So Jesus cast out the demon, and then the man began to speak. The crowds were amazed. "Nothing like this has ever happened in Israel!" they exclaimed.

But the Pharisees said, "He can cast out demons because he is empowered by the prince of demons."

Jesus left that part of the country and returned with his disciples to Nazareth, his hometown. The next Sabbath he began teaching in the synagogue, and many who heard him were amazed. They asked, "Where did he get all this wisdom and the power to perform such miracles?" Then they scoffed, "He's just a carpenter, the son of Mary and the brother of James, Joseph, Judas, and Simon. And his sisters live right here among us." They were deeply offended and refused to believe in him.

Then Jesus told them, "A prophet is honored everywhere except in his own hometown and among his relatives and his own family." And because of their unbelief, he couldn't do any mighty miracles among them except to place his hands on a few sick people and heal them. And he was amazed at their unbelief.

Jesus has now returned to His hometown, but He will soon be returning to His travels and teaching. Although people agree with His teaching and are amazed at His works, they can't get past "who" He really is. Many of these folks knew Jesus as a baby, child, and young man. Maybe they babysat, changed His diapers, or taught Him in school. They just can't bring themselves to place their faith in Him as Lord. Like that of His brothers, their view will change after Jesus' resurrection. But for now, there isn't much for Jesus to do in a place where people aren't coming to Him for help. So He moves on with His disciples to begin His third tour through Galilee.

୧఼෨

Scripture References

Luke 7–8; Matthew 11:20–30; 12:22—13:58; 9:18–34; Mark 3:20—6:6

Reflection

How was Jesus treated in his home town?

How can you show people how Jesus is changing you? How do you give people around you the benefit and space to let Jesus change them?

Chapter 6

Jesus Calls for Commitment

Jesus continues to minister in Galilee. Now that He has thoroughly taught and demonstrated the healing power of God's Kingdom, the time has come for His disciples to also teach and heal. Jesus understands that He is only one man and in order for His Gospel to expand, He will need others to go out on His behalf and reveal this new Kingdom to the world.

Jesus traveled through all the towns and villages of that area, teaching in the synagogues and announcing the Good News about the Kingdom. And he healed every kind of disease and illness. When he saw the crowds, he had compassion on them because they were confused and helpless, like sheep without a shepherd. He said to his disciples, "The harvest is great, but the workers are few. So pray to the Lord who is in charge of the harvest; ask him to send more workers into his fields."

Jesus called his twelve disciples together and began sending them out two by two, giving them power and authority to cast out evil spirits and to heal every kind of disease and illness. Then he sent them out to tell everyone about the Kingdom of God and to heal the sick.

Here are the names of the twelve apostles: first, Simon (also called Peter), then Andrew (Peter's brother), James (son of Zebedee), John (James's brother), Philip, Bartholomew, Thomas, Matthew (the tax collector), James (son of Alphaeus),

Thaddaeus, Simon (the zealot), Judas Iscariot (who later betrayed him).

Jesus sent out the twelve apostles with these instructions: "Don't go to the Gentiles or the Samaritans,[23] but only to the people of Israel—God's lost sheep. Go and announce to them that the Kingdom of Heaven[24] is near. Heal the sick, raise the dead, cure those with leprosy, and cast out demons. Give as freely as you have received!

"Don't take any money in your money belts—no gold, silver, or even copper coins. Don't carry a traveler's bag with a change of clothes and sandals or even a walking stick. Don't hesitate to accept hospitality, because those who work deserve to be fed.

"Whenever you enter a city or village, search for a worthy person and stay in his home until you leave town. When you enter the home, give it your blessing. If it turns out to be a worthy home, let your blessing stand; if it is not, take back the blessing. If any household or town refuses to welcome you or listen to your message, shake its dust from your feet

---

[23] **Gentiles or the Samaritans:** Jesus' ministry was first to the Jews, and then to the Gentiles (though ministry to the Gentiles would eventually evolve after the resurrection). Unlike the region of Judea, in which Jerusalem was located, Samaria was not predominantly occupied by Jews and therefore it was often thought of as unclean, even reprehensive.

[24] **Kingdom of Heaven:** Throughout the Gospels "Kingdom of Heaven" is interchangeable with "Kingdom of God." It is forbidden to speak God's name in Judaism, and because of Matthew's predominantly Jewish audience, substituting "heaven" for "God" is a more acceptable term to traditionalists.

as you leave to show that you have abandoned those people to their fate. I tell you the truth, the wicked cities of Sodom and Gomorrah will be better off than such a town on the judgment day.

"Look, I am sending you out as sheep among wolves. So be as shrewd as snakes and harmless as doves. But beware! For you will be handed over to the courts and will be flogged with whips in the synagogues. You will stand trial before governors and kings because you are my followers. But this will be your opportunity to tell the rulers and other unbelievers about me. When you are arrested, don't worry about how to respond or what to say. God will give you the right words at the right time. For it is not you who will be speaking—it will be the Spirit of your Father speaking through you.

"A brother will betray his brother to death, a father will betray his own child, and children will rebel against their parents and cause them to be killed. And all nations will hate you because you are my followers. But everyone who endures to the end will be saved. When you are persecuted in one town, flee to the next. I tell you the truth, the Son of Man will return before you have reached all the towns of Israel.

"Students are not greater than their teacher, and slaves are not greater than their master. Students are to be like their teacher, and slaves are to be like their master. And since I, the master of the household, have been called the prince of demons, the members of my household will be called by even worse names!

"But don't be afraid of those who threaten you. For the time is coming when everything that is covered will be revealed, and all that is secret will be made known to all. What I tell you now in the darkness, shout abroad when daybreak comes. What I whisper in your ear, shout from the housetops for all to hear!

"Don't be afraid of those who want to kill your body; they cannot touch your soul. Fear only God, who can destroy both soul and body in hell. What is the price of two sparrows—one copper coin? But not a single sparrow can fall to the ground without your Father knowing it. And the very hairs on your head are all numbered. So don't be afraid; you are more valuable to God than a whole flock of sparrows.

"Everyone who acknowledges me publicly here on earth, I will also acknowledge before my Father in heaven. But everyone who denies me here on earth, I will also deny before my Father in heaven."

Jesus expects His followers to willingly forfeit everything that separates us from the Gospel, even our very own flesh and blood. But alongside this challenge comes Jesus' promise that if we stand up for God's truth, Jesus will stand up for us. God will never abandon us; He will remain forever loyal.

"Don't imagine that I came to bring peace to the earth! I came not to bring peace, but a sword. From now on families will be split apart, three in favor of me, and two against—or two in favor and three against.

'I have come to set a man against his father, a daughter against her mother, and a daughter-in-law against her mother-in-law. Your enemies will be right in your own household!'

"If you love your father or mother more than you love me, you are not worthy of being mine; or if you love your son or daughter more than me, you are not worthy of being mine. If you refuse to take up your cross daily and follow me, you are not worthy of being mine. If you cling to your life, you will lose it; but if you give up your life for me, you will find it.

"Anyone who receives you receives me, and anyone who receives me receives the Father who sent me. If you receive a prophet as one who speaks for God, you will be given the same reward as a prophet. And if you receive righteous people because of their righteousness, you will be given a reward like theirs. And if you give even a cup of cold water to one of the least of my followers, you will surely be rewarded."

So the disciples went out, telling everyone they met to repent of their sins and turn to God. And they cast out many demons and healed many sick people, anointing them with olive oil.

Reflection

Notice Jesus does not try to do all the work on his own. Who does he rely on to help?

How are you involved in the harvest?

Even with Jesus' power and authority clearly on display, many of His followers remain ignorant of His true identity as God in flesh—even His own disciples. As Jesus continues to reveal Himself to those with eyes to see, another situation is developing with King Herod. Herod hears so much about Jesus that he wants to meet Jesus for himself. Herod Antipas, the king,[25] soon heard

25 **Herod Antipas, the king**: King Herod was a "tetrarch," which means he ruled over a fourth of the region of Palestine— more specifically, Judea and Perea. Herod

[Handwritten notes:]

His Twelve disciples. Apostles.

I pray to God, Jesus Christ my Lord and Savior and the Holy Spirit every day for my family relatives friends, Neighbors and my Church family and friends. I read

about Jesus, because everyone was talking about him; he was puzzled. Some were saying, "This must be John the Baptist raised from the dead. That is why he can do such miracles." Others said, "He's the prophet Elijah." Still others said, "He's a prophet like the other great prophets of the past."

When Herod heard about Jesus, he said, "John, the man I beheaded, has come back from the dead." And he kept trying to see him.

For Herod had sent soldiers to arrest and imprison John as a favor to Herodias. She had been his brother Philip's wife, but Herod had married her. John had been telling Herod, "It is against God's law for you to marry your brother's wife." So Herodias bore a grudge against John and wanted to kill him. But without Herod's approval she was powerless, for Herod respected John; and knowing that he was a good and holy man, he protected him. Herod was greatly disturbed whenever he talked with John, but even so, he liked to listen to him.

Herodias's chance finally came on Herod's birthday. He gave a party for his high government officials, army officers, and the leading citizens of Galilee. Then his daughter, also named Herodias, came in and performed a dance that greatly pleased Herod and his guests. "Ask me for anything you like," the king said to the girl, "and I will give it to you." He even vowed, "I will give you whatever you ask, up to half my kingdom!"

---

lacked absolute control over his region (as exemplified in the trial of Jesus), but he did have the power to maintain peace.

She went out and asked her mother, "What should I ask for?"

Her mother told her, "Ask for the head of John the Baptist!"

Reflection

🖐 Why is John in prison? How does Herodias get what she wants?

💜 Ponder what tempts you, who influences you and which situations are potentially harmful. What is your gameplan when you encounter these?

So the girl hurried back to the king and told him, "I want the head of John the Baptist, right now, on a tray!"

Then the king deeply regretted what he had said; but because of the vows he had made in front of his guests, he couldn't refuse her. So he immediately sent an executioner to the prison to cut off John's head and bring it to him. The soldier beheaded John in the prison, brought his head on a tray, and gave it to the girl, who took it to her mother. When John's disciples heard what had happened, they came to get his body and buried it in a tomb. Then they went and told Jesus what had happened.

⚜

In direct contrast to Herod's drunken and bloodthirsty festivities stand Jesus' compassion, power, and provision. Jesus is at the height of His popularity and is about to perform one of His most amazing miracles—the feeding of the 5,000.

The apostles returned to Jesus from their ministry tour and told him all they had done and taught. Then Jesus said, "Let's go off by ourselves to a quiet place and rest awhile." He said this because there were so many people coming and going that Jesus and his apostles didn't even have time to eat.

So they left by boat for a quiet place toward the town of Bethsaida, where they could be alone. But many people recognized them and saw them leaving, and people from many towns ran ahead along the shore and got there ahead of them. Jesus saw the huge crowd as he stepped from the boat, and he had compassion on them because they were like sheep without a shepherd. So he climbed a hill and sat down with his disciples around him and began teaching them many things about the Kingdom of God, and he healed those who were sick. (It was nearly time for the Jewish Passover celebration.) Jesus soon saw a huge crowd of people coming to look for him. Turning to Philip, he asked, "Where can we buy bread to feed all these people?" He was testing Philip, for he already knew what he was going to do.

Philip replied, "Even if we worked for months, we wouldn't have enough money to feed them!"

Late in the afternoon his disciples came to him and said, "This is a remote place, and it's already getting late. Send the crowds away so they can go to the nearby farms and villages, so they can find food and lodging for the night."

But Jesus said, "You feed them."

"With what?" they asked. "We'd have to work for months to earn enough money to buy food for all these people!"

"How much bread do you have?" he asked. "Go and find out."

They came back and Andrew, Simon Peter's brother, spoke up. "There's a young boy here with five barley loaves and two fish. But what good is that with this huge crowd? Or are you expecting us to go and buy enough food for this whole crowd?"

"Bring them here," Jesus said, "and tell everyone to sit down." So the people all sat down in groups of fifty or a hundred on the grassy slopes. Then Jesus took the five loaves, looked up to heaven, gave thanks to God, and distributed them to the people. Afterward he did the same with the two fish. And they all ate as much as they wanted. After everyone was full, Jesus told his disciples, "Now gather the leftovers, so that nothing is wasted." So they picked up the pieces and filled twelve baskets with scraps left by the people who had eaten from the five barley loaves. About 5,000 men[26] were fed that day, in addition to all the women and children!

When the people saw him do this miraculous sign, they exclaimed, "Surely, he is the Prophet we have been expecting!"

Immediately after this, Jesus insisted that his disciples get back into the boat and cross to the other side of the lake, while he sent the people home.

When Jesus saw that they were ready to force him to be their king, he slipped away into the hills by himself to pray.

Reflection

How does Jesus view others who need help?

How do you respond when to the needs of others? What about when you need help-how do you respond?

Late that night, the disciples were in their boat in the middle of the lake, and Jesus was alone on land. He saw that they were in serious trouble, rowing hard and struggling against the wind and waves. About three o'clock in the morning Jesus came toward them, walking on the water. He

---

[26] **5,000 men**: Only men were counted. With the women and children in attendance, it is entirely likely 15,000 people were fed.

intended to go past them, but when they saw him walking on the water, they were terrified. In their fear, they cried out, "It's a ghost!"

But Jesus spoke to them at once. "Don't be afraid," he said. "Take courage. I am here!"

Then Peter called to him, "Lord, if it's really you, tell me to come to you, walking on the water."

"Yes, come," Jesus said.

So Peter went over the side of the boat and walked on the water toward Jesus. But when he saw the strong wind and the waves, he was terrified and began to sink. "Save me, Lord!" he shouted.

Jesus immediately reached out and grabbed him. "You have so little faith," Jesus said. "Why did you doubt me?"

When they climbed back into the boat, the wind stopped. Then the disciples worshiped him. "You really are the Son of God!" they exclaimed. They were totally amazed, for they still didn't understand the significance of the miracle of the loaves. Their hearts were too hard to take it in. Then immediately they arrived at their destination!

After they had crossed the lake, they landed at Gennesaret. They brought the boat to shore and climbed out. The people recognized Jesus at once, and they ran throughout the whole area, carrying sick people on mats to wherever they heard he was. Wherever he went—in villages, cities, or the countryside—they brought the sick out to the marketplaces. They begged him to let the sick touch at least the fringe of his robe, and all who touched him were healed.

Reflection

How did the disciples respond after all they had witnessed?

How can you encourage those who doubt? What do you do when you doubt?

The next day the crowd that had stayed on the far shore saw that the disciples had taken the only boat, and they realized Jesus had not gone with them. Several boats from Tiberias landed near the place where the Lord had blessed the bread and the people had eaten. So when the crowd saw that neither Jesus nor his disciples were there, they got into the boats and went across to Capernaum to look for him. They found him on the other side of the lake and asked, "Rabbi, when did you get here?"

Jesus replied, "I tell you the truth, you want to be with me because I fed you, not because you understood the miraculous signs. But don't be so concerned about perishable things like food. Spend your energy seeking the eternal life that the Son of Man can give you. For God the Father has given me the seal of his approval."

They replied, "We want to perform God's works, too. What should we do?"

Jesus told them, "This is the only work God wants from you: Believe in the one he has sent."

They answered, "Show us a miraculous sign if you want us to believe in you. What can you do? After all, our ancestors ate manna while they journeyed through the wilderness! The Scriptures say, 'Moses gave them bread from heaven to eat.' "

Jesus said, "I tell you the truth, Moses didn't give you bread from heaven. My Father did. And now he offers you the true bread from heaven. The true bread of God is the one who comes down from heaven and gives life to the world."

"Sir," they said, "give us that bread every day."

Jesus replied, "I am the bread of life. Whoever comes to me will never be hungry again. Whoever believes in me will never be thirsty. But you haven't believed in me even though you have seen me. However, those the Father has given me will come to me, and I will never reject them. For I have come down from heaven to do the will of God who sent me, not to do my own will. And this is the will of God, that I should not lose even one of all those he has given me, but that I should raise them up at the last day. For it is my Father's will that all who see his Son and believe in him should have eternal life. I will raise them up at the last day."

Then the people began to murmur in disagreement because he had said, "I am the bread that came down from heaven." They said, "Isn't this Jesus, the son of Joseph? We know his father and mother. How can he say, 'I came down from heaven'?"

But Jesus replied, "Stop complaining about what I said. For no one can come to me unless the Father who sent me draws them to me, and at the last day I will raise them up. As it is written in the Scriptures, 'They will all be taught by God.' Everyone who listens to the Father and learns from him comes to me. (Not that anyone has ever seen the Father; only I, who was sent from God, have seen him.)

"I tell you the truth, anyone who believes has eternal life. Yes, I am the bread of life! Your ancestors ate manna in the wilderness, but they all died. Anyone who eats the bread from heaven, however, will never die. I am the living bread that came down from heaven. Anyone who eats this bread will live forever; and this bread, which I will offer so the world may live, is my flesh."

Then the people began arguing with each other
about what he meant. "How can this man give us his
flesh to eat?" they asked.

So Jesus said again, "I tell you the truth, unless
you eat the flesh of the Son of Man and drink his
blood, you cannot have eternal life within you. But
anyone who eats my flesh and drinks my blood has
eternal life, and I will raise that person at the last day.
For my flesh is true food, and my blood is true
drink. Anyone who eats my flesh and drinks my
blood remains in me, and I in him. I live because of
the living Father who sent me; in the same way,
anyone who feeds on me will live because of me. I
am the true bread that came down from heaven.
Anyone who eats his bread will not die as your
ancestors did (even though they ate the manna) but
will live forever."

He said these things while he was teaching in
the synagogue in Capernaum.

Many of his disciples said, "This is very hard to
understand. How can anyone accept it?"

Jesus was aware that his disciples were complaining, so he said to them, "Does this offend you?
Then what will you think if you see the Son of Man
ascend to heaven again? The Spirit alone gives
eternal life. Human effort accomplishes nothing.
And the very words I have spoken to you are spirit
and life. But some of you do not believe me." (For
Jesus knew from the beginning which ones didn't
believe, and he knew who would betray him.) Then
he said, "That is why I said that people can't come
to me unless the Father gives them to me."

At this point many of his disciples turned away and deserted him. Then Jesus turned to the Twelve and asked, "Are you also going to leave?"

Simon Peter replied, "Lord, to whom would we go? You have the words that give eternal life. We believe, and we know you are the Holy One of God."

Then Jesus said, "I chose the twelve of you, but one is a devil." He was speaking of Judas, son of Simon Iscariot, one of the Twelve, who would later betray him.

The people want a political messiah, but Jesus offers something much deeper. Because Jesus teaches truth, His teachings attract and frustrate His listeners, depending on if they like the message or not. But Jesus isn't running for office, He is revealing the only way to true and eternal life.

Reflection

How did Jesus weed out those who were following him for personal gain?

Are there parts of scripture that are harder for you to accept and follow? How do you come to terms with those parts?

Scripture References

Matthew 9:35—11:1; 14:1–36; Mark 6:6–56; Luke 9:1–17; John 6

Third Year of His Mission

Travels in the Third Year of His Mission

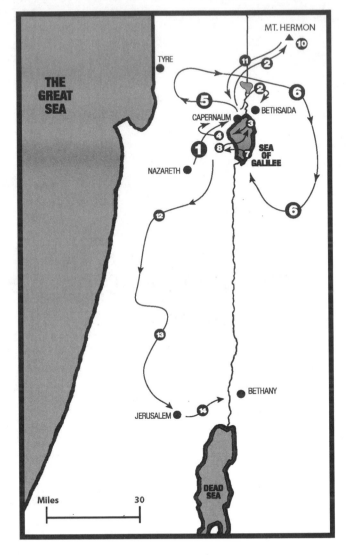

1. From Nazareth through the Galilean towns and villages, to Capernaum.

2. From Capernaum to the desert near Bethsaida.

3. From the desert near Bethsaida to Gennesaret.

4. From Gennesaret to Capernaum.

5. From Capernaum to Phoenicia.

6. From Phoenicia through Decapolis.

7. From Decapolis, by boat, to Dalmanutha.

8. From Dalmanutha, by boat, to Bethsaida.

9. From Bethsaida to Caesarea Philippi.

10. From Caesarea Philippi to the mountain where Jesus was transformed.

11. From the the mountain where Jesus was transformed to Capernaum.

12. From Capernaum through Samaria.

13. From Samaria to Jerusalem.

14. From Jerusalem to Bethany across Jordan.

Chapter 7

Jesus Trains His Disciples

Feeding the 5,000 followed by the sermon on bread stir things up once again with the religious authorities and this time the crowds seem bothered too. Many decide to leave Jesus because His teaching is just too hard and now the Jewish leaders are so upset that they want to do away with Jesus altogether.

After this, Jesus traveled around Galilee. He wanted to stay out of Judea, where the Jewish leaders were plotting his death.

One day some Pharisees and teachers of religious law arrived from Jerusalem to see Jesus. They noticed that some of his disciples failed to follow the Jewish ritual of hand washing before eating. (The Jews, especially the Pharisees, do not eat until they have poured water over their cupped hands, as required by their ancient traditions. Similarly, they don't eat anything from the market until they immerse their hands in water. This is but one of many traditions they have clung to—such as their ceremonial washing of cups, pitchers, and kettles.)

So the Pharisees and teachers of religious law asked him, "Why don't your disciples follow our age-old tradition? They eat without first performing the hand-washing ceremony."

Jesus replied, "You hypocrites! Isaiah was right when he prophesied about you, for he wrote,

' These people honor me with their lips,
but their hearts are far from me. Their

worship is a farce, for they teach man-made ideas as commands from God.'

For you ignore God's law and substitute your own tradition."

Then he said, "You skillfully sidestep God's law in order to hold on to your own tradition. For instance, Moses gave you this law from God: 'Honor your father and mother,' and 'Anyone who speaks disrespectfully of father or mother must be put to death.' But you say it is all right for people to say to their parents, 'Sorry, I can't help you. For I have vowed to give to God what I would have given to you.' In this way, you let them disregard their needy parents. And so you cancel the word of God in order to hand down your own tradition. And this is only one example among many others."

Then Jesus called to the crowd to come and hear. "Listen," he said, "and try to understand. It's not what goes into your mouth that defiles you; you are defiled by the words that come out of your mouth."

Then the disciples came to him and asked, "Do you realize you offended the Pharisees by what you just said?"

Jesus replied, "Every plant not planted by my heavenly Father will be uprooted, so ignore them. They are blind guides leading the blind, and if one blind person guides another, they will both fall into a ditch."

Then Jesus went into the house to get away from the crowd, and Peter said to Jesus, "Explain to us the parable that says people aren't defiled by what they eat."

"Don't you understand yet?" Jesus asked. "Anything you eat passes through the stomach and then goes into the sewer. But the words you speak come from the heart—that's what defiles you. (By saying this, he declared that every kind of food is acceptable in God's eyes.)

And then he added, "It is what comes from inside that defiles you. For from within, out of a person's heart, come evil thoughts, sexual immorality, theft, murder, adultery, greed, wickedness, deceit, lustful desires, envy, slander, pride, and foolishness. All these vile things come from within; they are what defile you. Eating with unwashed hands will never defile you."

Jesus always elevates the motives of our heart above religious activity. In this exchange about eating, He's not just talking about how to treat food; He's also talking about how to treat people. Jesus illustrates this through his extravagant compassion. Notably, He encounters a woman who was all wrong according to external standards. But her heart of faith more than makes up for any of her perceived shortcomings.

Reflection

Why do you think the disciples asked Jesus if he realized that he was offending the Pharisees?

What things cause you to wonder if Jesus really understands the impact of what he is doing in your life?

Then Jesus left Galilee and went north to the region of Tyre and Sidon. He didn't want anyone to know which house he was staying in, but he couldn't keep it a secret. Right away a Gentile woman, born in Syrian Phoenicia, who lived in the region of Tyre and Sidon, came to him, pleading, "Have mercy on me, O Lord, Son of David! For my daughter is possessed by a demon that torments her severely."

But Jesus gave her no reply, not even a word. Then his disciples urged him to send her away. "Tell her to go away," they said. "She is bothering us with all her begging." Then Jesus said to the woman, "I was sent only to help God's lost sheep—the people of Israel.[27]"

But she came and worshiped him, pleading again, "Lord, help me!" And she begged him to cast out the demon from her daughter.

Jesus responded, "First I should feed the children—my own family, the Jews. It isn't right to take food from the children and throw it to the dogs."

She replied, "That's true, Lord, but even the dogs under the table are allowed to eat the scraps from the children's plates."

"Good answer! Your faith is great," he said. "Your request is granted. Now go home, for the demon has left your daughter." And her daughter was instantly healed. When she arrived home, she found her little girl lying quietly in bed, and the demon was gone.

Jesus left Tyre and went up to Sidon before going back to the Sea of Galilee and the region of the Ten Towns and climbed a hill and sat down. A deaf man with a speech impediment was brought to

---

[27] This seems to be an odd response from Jesus since He is usually quick to help the down and out. However, Jesus was sent to the Jews first and then the message was to go out from there. By saying He was sent only to the Jews but also helping this non-Jewish woman, Jesus models an important principle for His disciples. Even though the initial strategy is for Jesus to go to the Jews first, the ultimate plan is for the Kingdom of God to be offered to all people.

him, and the people begged Jesus to lay his hands on the man to heal him.

Jesus led him away from the crowd so they could be alone. He put his fingers into the man's ears. Then, spitting on his own fingers, he touched the man's tongue. Looking up to heaven, he sighed and said, *"Ephphatha,"* which means, "Be opened!" Instantly the man could hear perfectly, and his tongue was freed so he could speak plainly!

Jesus told the crowd not to tell anyone, but the more he told them not to, the more they spread the news. They were completely amazed and said again and again, "Everything he does is wonderful. He even makes the deaf to hear and gives speech to those who cannot speak."

A vast crowd brought to him people who were lame, blind, crippled, those who couldn't speak, and many others. They laid them before Jesus, and he healed them all. The crowd was amazed! Those who hadn't been able to speak were talking, the crippled were made well, the lame were walking, and the blind could see again! And they praised the God of Israel.

About this time another large crowd had gathered, and the people ran out of food again. Jesus called his disciples and told them, "I feel sorry for these people. They have been here with me for three days, and they have nothing left to eat. If I send them home hungry, they will faint along the way. For some of them have come a long distance."

His disciples replied, "How are we supposed to find enough food to feed them out here in the wilderness?"

Jesus asked, "How much bread do you have?"

"Seven loaves," they replied.

So Jesus told all the people to sit down on the ground. Then he took the seven loaves, thanked God for them, and broke them into pieces. He gave them to his disciples, who distributed the bread to the crowd. A few small fish were found, too, so Jesus also blessed these and told the disciples to distribute them.

They ate as much as they wanted. Afterward, the disciples picked up seven large baskets of leftover food. There were about 4,000 people in the crowd that day, in addition to all the women and children. Then Jesus sent the people home, and he got into a boat and crossed over to the region of Magadan.

After feeding the 4,000 in the region of the Ten Towns, Jesus returns to Jewish territory, where He is hassled by the Pharisees and Sadducees. The questions aren't new; they've been asked at least three different times by the same group. This only provides more proof that the Pharisees aren't sincere in their spiritual search; they are only trying to trap Jesus. Not only will Jesus continue His work; He will also begin to issue serious warnings about following these religious leaders.

One day the Pharisees and Sadducees came to test Jesus, demanding that he show them a miraculous sign from heaven to prove his authority.

He sighed deeply in his spirit and replied, "You know the saying, 'Red sky at night means fair weather tomorrow; red sky in the morning means foul weather all day.' You know how to interpret the weather signs in the sky, but you don't know how to interpret the signs of the times! So he got back into the boat and left them, and he crossed to the other side of the lake.

But the disciples had forgotten to bring any food. They had only one loaf of bread with them in the boat. As they were crossing the lake, Jesus warned them, "Watch out! Beware of the yeast of the Pharisees and Sadducees and of Herod."

At this they began to argue with each other because they hadn't brought any bread. Jesus knew what they were saying, so he said, "You have so little faith! Why are you arguing about having no bread? Don't you know or understand even yet? Are your hearts too hard to take it in? 'You have eyes—can't you see? You have ears—can't you hear?' Don't you remember anything at all? When I fed the 5,000 with five loaves of bread, how many baskets of leftovers did you pick up afterward?"

"Twelve," they said.

"And when I fed the 4,000 with seven loaves, how many large baskets of leftovers did you pick up?"

"Seven," they said.

"Don't you understand yet?" he asked them. "Why can't you understand that I'm not talking about bread? So again I say, 'Beware of the yeast of the Pharisees and Sadducees.'"

Then at last they understood that he wasn't speaking about the yeast in bread, but about the deceptive teaching of the Pharisees and Sadducees.

Reflection

How does Jesus respond to the Gentile woman's request to heal her daughter?

As you look at this Gentile woman how does she encourage you in your relationship with Jesus?

When they arrived at Bethsaida, some people brought a blind man to Jesus, and they begged him

[Handwritten marginal notes:] Jesus said, "First I should feed the children and my own family, the Jews. It isn't right to take food from the children and throw it to the dogs."

to touch the man and heal him. Jesus took the blind man by the hand and led him out of the village. Then, spitting on the man's eyes, he laid his hands on him and asked, "Can you see anything now?"

The man looked around. "Yes," he said, "I see people, but I can't see them very clearly. They look like trees walking around."

Then Jesus placed his hands on the man's eyes again, and his eyes were opened. His sight was completely restored, and he could see everything clearly. Jesus sent him away, saying, "Don't go back into the village on your way home."

When Jesus came to the region of Caesarea Philippi, as they were walking along he asked his disciples, "Who do people say that the Son of Man is?"

"Well," they replied, "some say John the Baptist, some say Elijah, and others say Jeremiah or one of the other prophets risen from the dead."

Then he asked them, "But who do you say I am?"

Simon Peter answered, "You are the Messiah, the Son of the living God."

Jesus replied, "You are blessed, Simon son of John, because my Father in heaven has revealed this to you. You did not learn this from any human being. Now I say to you that you are Peter (which means 'rock'), and upon this rock I will build my church, and all the powers of hell will not conquer it. And I will give you the keys of the Kingdom of Heaven. Whatever you forbid on earth will be forbidden in heaven, and whatever you permit on earth will be permitted in heaven."

Then he sternly warned the disciples not to tell anyone that he was the Messiah.

From then on Jesus began to tell his disciples plainly that it was necessary for him to go to Jerusalem, and that he would suffer many terrible things and be rejected by the elders, the leading priests, and the teachers of religious law. He would be killed, but on the third day he would be raised from the dead.

As he talked about this openly with his disciples, Peter took him aside and began to reprimand him for saying such things. "Heaven forbid, Lord," he said. "This will never happen to you!"

Jesus turned around and looked at his disciples, then reprimanded Peter. "Get away from me, Satan!" he said. "You are a dangerous trap to me. You are seeing things merely from a human point of view, not from God's."

Then, calling the crowd to join his disciples, he said, "If any of you wants to be my follower, you must turn from your selfish ways, take up your cross daily, and follow me. If you try to hang on to your life, you will lose it. But if you give up your life for my sake and for the sake of the Good News, you will save it. And what do you benefit if you gain the whole world but lose your own soul? Is anything worth more than your soul? If anyone is ashamed of me and my message in these adulterous and sinful days, the Son of Man will be ashamed of that person when he returns in the glory of his Father with the holy angels. For the Son of Man will come with his angels in the glory of his Father and will judge all people according to their deeds."

Jesus went on to say, "I tell you the truth, some standing here right now will not die before they see the Kingdom of God arrive in great power!"

About eight days later Jesus took Peter, James, and John up on a high mountain to be alone and pray. And as he was praying, the appearance of his face was transformed so that his face shone like the sun, and his clothes became dazzling white, far whiter than any earthly bleach could ever make them. Suddenly, two men, Moses and Elijah, appeared and began talking with Jesus. They were glorious to see. And they were speaking about his exodus from this world, which was about to be fulfilled in Jerusalem.

Peter and the others had fallen asleep. When they woke up, they saw Jesus' glory and the two men standing with him. As Moses and Elijah were starting to leave, Peter blurted out, "Lord, it's wonderful for us to be here! If you want, I'll make three shelters as memorials— one for you, one for Moses, and one for Elijah." He said this because he didn't really know what else to say, for they were all terrified.

But even as he spoke, a bright cloud came over them, and a voice from the cloud said, "This is my dearly loved Son, who brings me great joy. Listen to him." The disciples were terrified and fell face down on the ground.

Then Jesus came over and touched them. "Get up," he said. "Don't be afraid." And when they looked, they saw only Jesus.

As they went back down the mountain, Jesus commanded them, "Don't tell anyone what you have seen until the Son of Man has been raised from the dead." So they kept it to themselves, but they often asked each other what he meant by "rising from the dead."

Then his disciples asked him, "Why do the teachers of religious law insist that Elijah must return before the Messiah comes?"

Jesus replied, "Elijah is indeed coming first to get everything ready for the Messiah. Yet why do the Scriptures say that the Son of Man must suffer greatly and be treated with utter contempt? But I tell you, Elijah has already come, but he wasn't recognized, and they chose to abuse him. And in the same way they will also make the Son of Man suffer." Then the disciples realized he was talking about John the Baptist.

Reflection

 What did Jesus ask his disciples? How did they respond?

How would you respond to Jesus' question? How is your understanding of who Jesus is impacting your family? Your other relationships?

What an incredible week of ups and downs for Jesus and His followers! The religious leaders are still harassing them, but that doesn't stop Peter from making "the good confession," upon which Jesus will build the church! But no sooner do these glorious words roll off of Peter's lips, than he is foolishly rebuking Jesus. Jesus' response, "Get away from me, Satan," makes you wonder if it's the same guy who made such a wonderful confession. However, even this doesn't stop Jesus from taking Peter, James and John up the mountain to witness His trans-figuration—which is a preview of His resurrection. They need to know that even though Jesus will suffer and die, He will be resurrected and transformed. It's a mountaintop experience they will never forget! Then again, as they say, what goes up must come down . . . and when they do . . .

The next day, after they had come down the mountain, they saw a large crowd surrounding the other disciples, and some teachers of religious law were arguing with them. When the crowd saw Jesus, they were overwhelmed with awe, and they ran to greet him.

"What is all this arguing about?" Jesus asked.

One of the men in the crowd spoke up and said, "Lord, have mercy on my son. I brought my son, my only child, so you could heal him. He is possessed by an evil spirit that won't let him talk. And whenever this spirit seizes him, it throws him violently to the ground, making him scream. Then he foams at the mouth and grinds his teeth and becomes rigid. It batters him and hardly ever leaves him alone. So I asked your disciples to cast out the evil spirit, but they couldn't heal him."

Jesus said to them, "You faithless and corrupt people! How long must I be with you? How long must I put up with you? Bring the boy to me."

So they brought the boy. But when the evil spirit saw Jesus, it threw the child into a violent convulsion, and he fell to the ground, writhing and foaming at the mouth.

"How long has this been happening?" Jesus asked the boy's father.

He replied, "Since he was a little boy. The spirit often throws him into the fire or into water, trying to kill him. Have mercy on us and help us, if you can."

"What do you mean, 'If I can'?" Jesus asked. "Anything is possible if a person believes."

The father instantly cried out, "I do believe, but help me overcome my unbelief!"

When Jesus saw that the crowd of onlookers was growing, he rebuked the evil spirit. "Listen, you spirit that makes this boy unable to hear and speak," he said. "I command you to come out of this child and never enter him again!"

Then the spirit screamed and threw the boy into another violent convulsion and left him. The boy appeared to be dead. A murmur ran through the crowd as people said, "He's dead." But Jesus took him by the hand and helped him to his feet, and he stood up. From that moment the boy was well and then Jesus gave him back to his father. Awe gripped the people as they saw this majestic display of God's power.

Afterward, when Jesus was alone in the house with his disciples, they asked him, "Why couldn't we cast out that evil spirit?"

"You don't have enough faith," Jesus told them. "I tell you the truth, if you had faith even as small as a mustard seed, you could say to this mountain, 'Move from here to there,' and it would move. Nothing would be impossible. This kind can be cast out only by prayer."

Leaving that region, they traveled through Galilee. Jesus didn't want anyone to know he was there, for he wanted to spend more time with his disciples and teach them. He said to them, "The Son of Man is going to be betrayed into the hands of his enemies. He will be killed, but three days later he will rise from the dead." They didn't understand what he was saying, however, and they were afraid to ask him what he meant. And the disciples were filled with grief.

On their arrival in Capernaum, the collectors of the Temple tax came to Peter and asked him, "Doesn't your teacher pay the Temple tax?"

"Yes, he does," Peter replied. Then he went into the house.

But before he had a chance to speak, Jesus asked him, "What do you think, Peter? Do kings tax their own people or the people they have conquered?"

"They tax the people they have conquered," Peter replied.

"Well, then," Jesus said, "the citizens are free! However, we don't want to offend them, so go down to the lake and throw in a line. Open the mouth of the first fish you catch, and you will find a large silver coin. Take it and pay the tax for both of us."

After they arrived at Capernaum and settled in a house, the disciples came to Jesus and asked, "Who is the greatest in the Kingdom of Heaven?"

Jesus asked his disciples, "What were you discussing out on the road?" But they didn't answer, because they had been arguing about which of them was the greatest. He sat down, called the twelve disciples over to him, and said, "Whoever wants to be first must take last place and be the servant of everyone else."

But Jesus knew their thoughts, so he brought a little child to him and put the child among them. Then he said, "I tell you the truth, unless you turn from your sins and become like little children, you will never get into the Kingdom of Heaven. So anyone who becomes as humble as this little child is the greatest in the Kingdom of Heaven."

Then he said to them, "Anyone who welcomes
a little child like this on my behalf welcomes me, and
anyone who welcomes me also welcomes my Father
who sent me. Whoever is the least among you is the
greatest."

John said to Jesus, "Teacher, we saw someone
using your name to cast out demons, but we told
him to stop because he wasn't in our group."

"Don't stop him!" Jesus said. "No one who
performs a miracle in my name will soon be able to
speak evil of me. Anyone who is not against us is for
us. If anyone gives you even a cup of water because
you belong to the Messiah, I tell you the truth, that
person will surely be rewarded.

"But if you cause one of these little ones who
trusts in me to fall into sin, it would be better for
you to have a large millstone tied around your neck
and be drowned in the depths of the sea.

"What sorrow awaits the world, because it
tempts people to sin. Temptations are inevitable, but
what sorrow awaits the person who does the
tempting. So if your hand or foot causes you to sin,
cut it off and throw it away. It's better to enter
eternal life with only one hand or one foot than to
be thrown into eternal fire with both of your hands
and feet. And if your eye causes you to sin, gouge it
out[28] and throw it away. It's better to enter eternal

---

[28] **cut it off . . . gouge it out**: Jesus is not promoting
actual physical mutilation. But he is promoting self-denial for
the sake of God's Kingdom. If looking at something or
someone unleashes desire that causes you to sin, Jesus says to
act as though your eyes are cut out. This is a call to radical
repentance. To show just how critical his point is, Jesus brings
up the subject of hell. The word for hell that Jesus uses is
"gehenna," the name of a valley south of Jerusalem. It was the

life with only one eye than to have two eyes and be thrown into the fire of hell, 'where the maggots never die and the fire never goes out.'

"For everyone will be tested with fire. Salt is good for seasoning. But if it loses its flavor, how do you make it salty again? You must have the qualities of salt among yourselves and live in peace with each other.

"Beware that you don't look down on any of these little ones. For I tell you that in heaven their angels are always in the presence of my heavenly Father.

"If a man has a hundred sheep and one of them wanders away, what will he do? Won't he leave the ninety-nine others on the hills and go out to search for the one that is lost? And if he finds it, I tell you the truth, he will rejoice over it more than over the ninety-nine that didn't wander away! In the same way, it is not my heavenly Father's will that even one of these little ones should perish. "If another believer sins against you, go privately and point out the offense. If the other person listens and confesses it, you have won that person back. But if you are unsuccessful, take one or two others with you and go back again, so that everything you say may be confirmed by two or three witnesses. If the person still refuses to listen, take your case to the church.

---

center of idol worship, including human sacrifice. King Josiah's reforms (2 Kings 23:10) turned it into a city dump where trash was burned, including human excrement and animal carcasses. Its stench was pervasive and the fire that burned seemed to never go out. This is the picture that Jesus paints about hell. Since hell is hot and it is eternal, it's better to deny our sinful desires than to suffer for all of eternity

Reflection

Jesus he-
aled a child
that his disci-
ples couldn't.
What was Je-
sus response
when they
asked him how
he was able to
heal the child?

How do
you view the
power of Jesus
in the presence
of evil? What
habits help you
be prepared to
engage the
world you live
in?

Then if he or she won't accept the church's decision, treat that person as a pagan or a corrupt tax collector.

"I tell you the truth, whatever you forbid on earth will be forbidden in heaven, and whatever you permit on earth will be permitted in heaven.

"I also tell you this: If two of you agree here on earth concerning anything you ask, my Father in heaven will do it for you. For where two or three gather together as my followers, I am there among them."

Then Peter came to him and asked, "Lord, how often should I forgive someone who sins against me? Seven times?"

"No, not seven times," Jesus replied, "but seventy times seven!

"Therefore, the Kingdom of Heaven can be compared to a king who decided to bring his accounts up to date with servants who had borrowed money from him. In the process, one of his debtors was brought in who owed him millions of dollars. He couldn't pay, so his master ordered that he be sold—along with his wife, his children, and everything he owned—to pay the debt. "But the man fell down before his master and begged him, 'Please, be patient with me, and I will pay it all.' Then his master was filled with pity for him, and he released him and forgave his debt.

"But when the man left the king, he went to a fellow servant who owed him a few thousand dollars. He grabbed him by the throat and demanded instant payment.

"His fellow servant fell down before him and begged for a little more time. 'Be patient with me, and I will pay it,' he pleaded. But his creditor wouldn't wait. He had the man arrested and put in prison until the debt could be paid in full.

"When some of the other servants saw this, they were very upset. They went to the king and told him everything that had happened. Then the king called in the man he had forgiven and said, 'You evil servant! I forgave you that tremendous debt because you pleaded with me. Shouldn't you have mercy on your fellow servant, just as I had mercy on you?' Then the angry king sent the man to prison to be tortured until he had paid his entire debt.

"That's what my heavenly Father will do to you if you refuse to forgive your brothers and sisters from your heart."

> *We live in a "live and let live" culture. What you do is your business, and what I do is mine. But God's Kingdom calls us to a much higher standard. Jesus commands us to care enough about the spiritual well-being of others to humbly go to them when they've offended us. The goal is restoration and reconciliation for those who have strayed. If done in humble love, it usually succeeds. But too often the problem isn't so much that the person being confronted won't listen, it's that the person who was offended hasn't forgiven. This is why Jesus tells us we are to forgive seventy times seven, which means as many times as necessary. This is what it takes to love others in God's Kingdom.*

But soon it was time for the Jewish Festival of Shelters,[29] and Jesus' brothers said to him, "Leave here and go to Judea, where your followers can see your miracles! You can't become famous if you hide like this! If you can do such wonderful things, show yourself to the world!" For even his brothers didn't believe in him.

Jesus replied, "Now is not the right time for me to go, but you can go anytime. The world can't hate you, but it does hate me because I accuse it of doing evil. You go on. I'm not going to this festival, because my time has not yet come." After saying these things, Jesus remained in Galilee.

As the time drew near for him to ascend to heaven, Jesus resolutely set out for Jerusalem. He sent messengers ahead to a Samaritan village to prepare for his arrival. But the people of the village did not welcome Jesus because he was on his way to Jerusalem. When James and John saw this, they said to Jesus, "Lord, should we call down fire from heaven to burn them up?" But Jesus turned and rebuked them. So they went on to another village.

Jesus was accepted in Samaria the first time He went, so it's unclear why He is rejected this time. James and John, dubbed Sons of Thunder, offer to take care of these ungrateful Samaritans for snubbing Jesus. Obviously, James and John

---

[29] **Festival of Shelters**: Also referred to as the Festival of Tabernacles, this festival is one of the three major Jewish feasts along with Passover and Pentecost. It was an eight-day festival that celebrated both the exodus from Egyptian slavery and God's provision for the Israelites during their wilderness wanderings. Shelters (tabernacles) were set up all over the city, where families would eat and sleep as a reminder of their wilderness dwellings (Leviticus 23:43).

missed the prior lessons on humility and forgiveness. Of course, Jesus corrects this ridiculous offer. Don't they realize that Jesus came to save and not destroy? But it's time to move on. One of the greatest Jewish holidays, the Festival of the Shelters, is about to begin.

Scripture References

Matthew 15–18; Mark 7–9; John 7:1–10; Luke 9:18–56

Reflection

What is Jesus teaching about forgiveness in His story?

Where in your life, family, fellow believers, workplace, or community is there a need for you to extend forgiveness or to seek forgiveness?

140

Chapter 8

Jesus Sends His Disciples Out

Jesus' brothers thought the Festival of Shelters would be a perfect platform for Jesus to show off His miracles. Since His life is being threatened, Jesus rejects their advice. He will suffer one day, but it's too early for Him to die and end His earthly ministry. So, He waits to secretly sneak into Jerusalem until after the festivities begin. Jesus uses the festival as the backdrop to reveal His authority, identity, and mission. But will He survive this visit?

But after his brothers left for the festival, Jesus also went, though secretly, staying out of public view.

The Jewish leaders tried to find him at the festival and kept asking if anyone had seen him. There was a lot of grumbling about him among the crowds. Some argued, "He's a good man," but others said, "He's nothing but a fraud who deceives the people." But no one had the courage to speak favorably about him in public, for they were afraid of getting in trouble with the Jewish leaders.

Then, midway through the festival, Jesus went up to the Temple and began to teach. The people were surprised when they heard him. "How does he know so much when he hasn't been trained?" they asked.

So Jesus told them, "My message is not my own; it comes from God who sent me. Anyone who wants to do the will of God will know whether my

teaching is from God or is merely my own. Those
who speak for themselves want glory only for
themselves, but a person who seeks to honor the
one who sent him speaks truth, not lies. Moses gave
you the law, but none of you obeys it! In fact, you
are trying to kill me."

The crowd replied, "You're demon possessed!
Who's trying to kill you?"

Jesus replied, "I did one miracle on the Sabbath,
and you were amazed. But you work on the Sabbath,
too, when you obey Moses' law of circumcision.
(Actu-ally, this tradition of circumcision began with
the patri-archs, long before the law of Moses.) For if
the correct time for circumcising your son falls on
the Sabbath, you go ahead and do it so as not to
break the law of Moses. So why should you be angry
with me for healing a man on the Sabbath? Look
beneath the surface so you can judge correctly."

Some of the people who lived in Jerusalem
started to ask each other, "Isn't this the man they are
trying to kill? But here he is, speaking in public, and
they say nothing to him. Could our leaders possibly
believe that he is the Messiah? But how could he be?
For we know where this man comes from. When
the Messiah comes, he will simply appear; no one
will know where he comes from."

While Jesus was teaching in the Temple, he
called out, "Yes, you know me, and you know where
I come from. But I'm not here on my own. The one
who sent me is true, and you don't know him. But I
know him because I come from him, and he sent me
to you." Then the leaders tried to arrest him; but no
one laid a hand on him, because his time had not yet
come.

Many among the crowds at the Temple believed in him. "After all," they said, "would you expect the Messiah to do more miraculous signs than this man has done?"

When the Pharisees heard that the crowds were whispering such things, they and the leading priests sent Temple guards to arrest Jesus. But Jesus told them, "I will be with you only a little longer. Then I will return to the one who sent me. You will search for me but not find me. And you cannot go where I am going."

The Jewish leaders were puzzled by this statement. "Where is he planning to go?" they asked. "Is he thinking of leaving the country and going to the Jews in other lands? Maybe he will even teach the Greeks! What does he mean when he says, 'You will search for me but not find me,' and 'You cannot go where I am going'?"

On the last day, the climax of the festival, Jesus stood and shouted to the crowds, "Anyone who is thirsty may come to me! Anyone who believes in me may come and drink! For the Scriptures declare, 'Rivers of living water will flow from his heart.'" (When he said "living water," he was speaking of the Spirit, who would be given to everyone believing in him. But the Spirit had not yet been given, because Jesus had not yet entered into his glory.)

When the crowds heard him say this, some of them declared, "Surely this man is the Prophet we've been expecting." Others said, "He is the Messiah." Still others said, "But he can't be! Will the Messiah come from Galilee? For the Scriptures clearly state that the Messiah will be born of the royal line of David, in Bethlehem, the village where King David was born." So the crowd was divided about him.

Some even wanted him arrested, but no one laid a hand on him.

When the Temple guards returned without having arrested Jesus, the leading priests and Pharisees demanded, "Why didn't you bring him in?"

"We have never heard anyone speak like this!" the guards responded.

"Have you been led astray, too?" the Pharisees mocked. "Is there a single one of us rulers or Pharisees who believes in him? This foolish crowd follows him, but they are ignorant of the law. God's curse is on them!"

Then Nicodemus, the leader who had met with Jesus earlier, spoke up. "Is it legal to convict a man before he is given a hearing?" he asked.

They replied, "Are you from Galilee, too? Search the Scriptures and see for yourself—no prophet ever comes from Galilee!"

Then the meeting broke up, and everybody went home.

Jesus returned to the Mount of Olives, but early the next morning he was back again at the Temple. A crowd soon gathered, and he sat down and taught them. As he was speaking, the teachers of religious law and the Pharisees brought a woman who had been caught in the act of adultery. They put her in front of the crowd.

"Teacher," they said to Jesus, "this woman was caught in the act of adultery. The law of Moses says to stone her. What do you say?"

They were trying to trap him into saying something they could use against him, but Jesus stooped down and wrote in the dust with his finger.

They kept demanding an answer, so he stood up again and said, "All right, but let the one who has never sinned throw the first stone!" Then he stooped down again and wrote in the dust.

When the accusers heard this, they slipped away one by one, beginning with the oldest, until only Jesus was left in the middle of the crowd with the woman. Then Jesus stood up again and said to the woman, "Where are your accusers? Didn't even one of them condemn you?"

"No, Lord," she said.

And Jesus said, "Neither do I. Go and sin no more."

Jesus spoke to the people once more and said, "I am the light of the world. If you follow me, you won't have to walk in darkness, because you will have the light that leads to life."

The Pharisees replied, "You are making those claims about yourself! Such testimony is not valid."

Jesus told them, "These claims are valid even though I make them about myself. For I know where I came from and where I am going, but you don't know this about me. You judge me by human standards, but I do not judge anyone. And if I did, my judgment would be correct in every respect because I am not alone. The Father who sent me is with me. Your own law says that if two people agree about something, their witness is accepted as fact. I am one witness, and my Father who sent me is the other."

"Where is your father?" they asked.

Jesus answered, "Since you don't know who I am, you don't know who my Father is. If you knew me, you would also know my Father." Jesus made these statements while he was teaching in the section of the Temple known as the Treasury. But he was not arrested, because his time had not yet come.

Later Jesus said to them again, "I am going away. You will search for me but will die in your sin. You cannot come where I am going."

The people asked, "Is he planning to commit suicide? What does he mean, 'You cannot come where I am going'?"

Jesus continued, "You are from below; I am from above. You belong to this world; I do not. That is why I said that you will die in your sins; for unless you believe that I AM who I claim to be, you will die in your sins."

"Who are you?" they demanded.

Jesus replied, "The one I have always claimed to be. I have much to say about you and much to condemn, but I won't. For I say only what I have heard from the one who sent me, and he is completely truthful." But they still didn't understand that he was talking about his Father.

So Jesus said, "When you have lifted up the Son of Man on the cross, then you will understand that I AM he. I do nothing on my own but say only what the Father taught me. And the one who sent me is with me—he has not deserted me. For I always do what pleases him." Then many who heard him say these things believed in him.

Jesus said to the people who believed in him, "You are truly my disciples if you remain faithful to my teachings. And you will know the truth, and the truth will set you free."

"But we are descendants of Abraham," they said. "We have never been slaves to anyone. What do you mean, 'You will be set free'?"

Jesus replied, "I tell you the truth, everyone who sins is a slave of sin. A slave is not a permanent member of the family, but a son is part of the family forever. So if the Son sets you free, you are truly free. Yes, I realize that you are descendants of Abraham. And yet some of you are trying to kill me because there's no room in your hearts for my message. I am telling you what I saw when I was with my Father. But you are following the advice of your father."

"Our father is Abraham!" they declared.

"No," Jesus replied, "for if you were really the children of Abraham, you would follow his example. Instead, you are trying to kill me because I told you the truth, which I heard from God. Abraham never did such a thing. No, you are imitating your real father."

They replied, "We aren't illegitimate children! God himself is our true Father."

Jesus told them, "If God were your Father, you would love me, because I have come to you from God. I am not here on my own, but he sent me. Why can't you understand what I am saying? It's because you can't even hear me! For you are the children of your father the devil, and you love to do the evil things he does. He was a murderer from the beginning. He has always hated the truth, because there is no truth in him. When he lies, it is consistent with his character; for he is a liar and the father of lies. So when I tell the truth, you just naturally don't believe me! Which of you can truthfully accuse me of sin? And since I am telling you the truth, why don't you believe me? Anyone who belongs to God listens gladly to the words of God. But you don't listen because you don't belong to God."

The people retorted, "You Samaritan devil! Didn't we say all along that you were possessed by a demon?"

"No," Jesus said, "I have no demon in me. For I honor my Father—and you dishonor me. And though I have no wish to glorify myself, God is going to glorify me. He is the true judge. I tell you the truth, anyone who obeys my teaching will never die!" The people said, "Now we know you are possessed by a demon. Even Abraham and the prophets died, but you say, 'Anyone who obeys my teaching will never die!' Are you greater than our father Abraham? He died, and so did the prophets. Who do you think you are?"

Jesus answered, "If I want glory for myself, it doesn't count. But it is my Father who will glorify me. You say, 'He is our God,' but you don't even know him. I know him. If I said otherwise, I would be as great a liar as you! But I do know him and obey him. Your father Abraham rejoiced as he looked forward to my coming. He saw it and was glad."

The people said, "You aren't even fifty years old. How can you say you have seen Abraham?"

Jesus answered, "I tell you the truth, before Abraham was even born, I AM!" At that point they picked up stones to throw at him. But Jesus was hidden from them and left the Temple.

Reflection

Explain Jesus' consistent message in your own words.

Who do you say Jesus is?

People take issue with a lot of what Jesus says.
He claims to be the light, but only God is the
source of light. Jesus claims that He is sent by the
Father from above, but only God can claim
residence in heaven. He even claims that He
existed before their father Abraham and that He
is God! Now, He is about to provide them with a
miraculous sign and heal the blind man. Can they
accept Jesus as the Son of God or will their
spiritual blindness prevent them from seeing the
light? As Jesus was walking along, he saw a man
who had been blind from birth. "Rabbi," his
disciples asked him, "why was this man born
blind? Was it because of his own sins or his
parents' sins?"

"It was not because of his sins or his parents'
sins," Jesus answered. "This happened so the power
of God could be seen in him. We must quickly carry
out the tasks assigned us by the one who sent us.
The night is coming, and then no one can work. But
while I am here in the world, I am the light of the
world."

Then he spit on the ground, made mud with the
saliva, and spread the mud over the blind man's eyes.
He told him, "Go wash yourself in the pool of
Siloam" (Siloam means "sent"). So the man went
and washed and came back seeing!

His neighbors and others who knew him as a
blind beggar asked each other, "Isn't this the man
who used to sit and beg?" Some said he was, and
others said, "No, he just looks like him!"

But the beggar kept saying, "Yes, I am the same
one!"

They asked, "Who healed you? What happened?"

He told them, "The man they call Jesus made mud and spread it over my eyes and told me, 'Go to the pool of Siloam and wash yourself.' So I went and washed, and now I can see!"

"Where is he now?" they asked.

"I don't know," he replied.

Then they took the man who had been blind to the Pharisees, because it was on the Sabbath that Jesus had made the mud and healed him. The Pharisees asked the man all about it. So he told them, "He put the mud over my eyes, and when I washed it away, I could see!"

Some of the Pharisees said, "This man Jesus is not from God, for he is working on the Sabbath." Others said, "But how could an ordinary sinner do such miraculous signs?" So there was a deep division of opinion among them.

Then the Pharisees again questioned the man who had been blind and demanded, "What's your opinion about this man who healed you?"

The man replied, "I think he must be a prophet."

The Jewish leaders still refused to believe the man had been blind and could now see, so they called in his parents. They asked them, "Is this your son? Was he born blind? If so, how can he now see?"

His parents replied, "We know this is our son and that he was born blind, but we don't know how he can see or who healed him. Ask him. He is old enough to speak for himself." His parents said this because they were afraid of the Jewish leaders, who

had announced that anyone saying Jesus was the
Messiah would be expelled from the synagogue.
That's why they said, "He is old enough. Ask him."

So for the second time they called in the man
who had been blind and told him, "God should get
the glory for this, because we know this man Jesus is
a sinner."

"I don't know whether he is a sinner," the man
replied. "But I know this: I was blind, and now I can
see!"

"But what did he do?" they asked. "How did he
heal you?"

"Look!" the man exclaimed. "I told you once.
Didn't you listen? Why do you want to hear it again?
Do you want to become his disciples, too?"

Then they cursed him and said, "You are his
disciple, but we are disciples of Moses! We know
God spoke to Moses, but we don't even know
where this man comes from."

"Why, that's very strange!" the man replied.
"He healed my eyes, and yet you don't know where
he comes from? We know that God doesn't listen to
sinners, but he is ready to hear those who worship
him and do his will. Ever since the world began, no
one has been able to open the eyes of someone born
blind. If this man were not from God, he couldn't
have done it."

"You were born a total sinner!" they answered.
"Are you trying to teach us?" And they threw him
out of the synagogue.

When Jesus heard what had happened, he
found the man and asked, "Do you believe in the
Son of Man?"

The man answered, "Who is he, sir? I want to believe in him."

"You have seen him," Jesus said, "and he is speaking to you!"

"Yes, Lord, I believe!" the man said. And he worshiped Jesus.

Then Jesus told him, "I entered this world to render judgment—to give sight to the blind and to show those who think they see that they are blind."

Some Pharisees who were standing nearby heard him and asked, "Are you saying we're blind?"

"If you were blind, you wouldn't be guilty," Jesus replied. "But you remain guilty because you claim you can see.

"I tell you the truth, anyone who sneaks over the wall of a sheepfold, rather than going through the gate, must surely be a thief and a robber! But the one who enters through the gate is the shepherd of the sheep. The gatekeeper opens the gate for him, and the sheep recognize his voice and come to him. He calls his own sheep by name and leads them out. After he has gathered his own flock, he walks ahead of them, and they follow him because they know his voice. They won't follow a stranger; they will run from him because they don't know his voice."

Those who heard Jesus use this illustration didn't understand what he meant, so he explained it to them: "I tell you the truth, I am the gate for the sheep. All who came before me were thieves and robbers. But the true sheep did not listen to them. Yes, I am the gate. Those who come in through me will be saved. They will come and go freely and will find good pastures. The thief's purpose is to steal and kill and destroy. My purpose is to give them a rich and satisfying life.

"I am the good shepherd. The good shepherd sacrifices his life for the sheep. A hired hand will run when he sees a wolf coming. He will abandon the sheep because they don't belong to him and he isn't their shepherd. And so the wolf attacks them and scatters the flock. The hired hand runs away because he's working only for the money and doesn't really care about the sheep.

"I am the good shepherd; I know my own sheep, and they know me, just as my Father knows me and I know the Father. So I sacrifice my life for the sheep.   I have other sheep, too, that are not in this sheepfold. I must bring them also. They will listen to my voice, and there will be one flock with one shepherd.

"The Father loves me because I sacrifice my life so I may take it back again. No one can take my life from me. I sacrifice it voluntarily. For I have the authority to lay it down when I want to and also to take it up again. For this is what my Father has commanded."

When he said these things, the people were again divided in their opinions about him. Some said, "He's demon possessed and out of his mind. Why listen to a man like that?" Others said, "This doesn't sound like a man possessed by a demon! Can a demon open the eyes of the blind?"

Has Jesus lost His mind? Doesn't He see that some people are perplexed and many are offended? But Jesus doesn't have time for being politically

Reflection

How did Jesus' interaction with the blind man impact various people?

Today many voices speak about being spiritual. Jesus speaks to us through His word. How do you hear His voice and follow Him?

correct. He now turns His focus to spreading His message even further by sending out seventy-two of His followers on mission. They are to announce the Good News: the Kingdom of God has come! But the Jewish leaders don't see it as good news as they continue looking for some way to set Jesus up for a big fall. So, Jesus gives these instructions to His missionary team.

As they were walking along, one of the teachers of religious law said to Jesus, "Teacher, I will follow you wherever you go."

But Jesus replied, "Foxes have dens to live in, and birds have nests, but the Son of Man has no place even to lay his head."

He said to another person, "Come, follow me." The man agreed, but he said, "Lord, first let me return home and bury my father."

But Jesus told him, "Follow me now. Let the spiritually dead bury their own dead! Your duty is to go and preach about the Kingdom of God."

Another said, "Yes, Lord, I will follow you, but first let me say good-bye to my family."

But Jesus told him, "Anyone who puts a hand to the plow and then looks back is not fit for the Kingdom of God."

The Lord now chose seventy-two other disciples and sent them ahead in pairs to all the towns and places he planned to visit. These were his instructions to them: "The harvest is great, but the workers are few. So pray to the Lord who is in charge of the harvest; ask him to send more workers into his fields. Now go, and remember that I am sending you out as lambs among wolves. Don't take any money with you, nor a traveler's bag, nor an extra pair of sandals. And don't stop to greet anyone on the road.

"Whenever you enter someone's home, first say, 'May God's peace be on this house.' If those who live there are peaceful, the blessing will stand; if they are not, the blessing will return to you. Don't move around from home to home. Stay in one place, eating and drinking what they provide. Don't hesitate to accept hospitality, because those who work deserve their pay.

"If you enter a town and it welcomes you, eat whatever is set before you. Heal the sick, and tell them, 'The Kingdom of God is near you now.' But if a town refuses to welcome you, go out into its streets and say, 'We wipe even the dust of your town from our feet to show that we have abandoned you to your fate. And know this—the Kingdom of God is near!' I assure you, even wicked Sodom will be better off than such a town on judgment day.

"What sorrow awaits you, Korazin and Bethsaida! For if the miracles I did in you had been done in wicked Tyre and Sidon, their people would have repented of their sins long ago, clothing themselves in burlap and throwing ashes on their heads to show their remorse. Yes, Tyre and Sidon will be better off on judgment day than you. And you people of Capernaum, will you be honored in heaven? No, you will go down to the place of the dead."

Then he said to the disciples, "Anyone who accepts your message is also accepting me. And anyone who rejects you is rejecting me. And anyone who rejects me is rejecting God, who sent me."

When the seventy-two disciples returned, they joyfully reported to him, "Lord, even the demons obey us when we use your name!"

"Yes," he told them, "I saw Satan fall from heaven like lightning! Look, I have given you authority over all the power of the enemy, and you can walk among snakes and scorpions and crush them. Nothing will injure you. But don't rejoice because evil spirits obey you; rejoice because your names are registered in heaven."

At that same time Jesus was filled with the joy of the Holy Spirit, and he said, "O Father, Lord of heaven and earth, thank you for hiding these things from those who think themselves wise and clever, and for revealing them to the childlike. Yes, Father, it pleased you to do it this way.

"My Father has entrusted everything to me. No one truly knows the Son except the Father, and no one truly knows the Father except the Son and those to whom the Son chooses to reveal him."

Then when they were alone, he turned to the disciples and said, "Blessed are the eyes that see what you have seen. I tell you, many prophets and kings longed to see what you see, but they didn't see it. And they longed to hear what you hear, but they didn't hear it."

One day an expert in religious law stood up to test Jesus by asking him this question: "Teacher, what should I do to inherit eternal life?"

Jesus replied, "What does the law of Moses say? How do you read it?"

The man answered, "'You must love the Lord your God with all your heart, all your soul, all your strength, and all your mind.' And, 'Love your neighbor as yourself.' "

"Right!" Jesus told him. "Do this and you will live!"

The man wanted to justify his actions, so he asked Jesus, "And who is my neighbor?"

Jesus replied with a story: "A Jewish man was traveling on a trip from Jerusalem to Jericho, and he was attacked by bandits. They stripped him of his clothes, beat him up, and left him half dead beside the road.

"By chance a priest came along. But when he saw the man lying there, he crossed to the other side of the road and passed him by. A Temple assistant walked over and looked at him lying there, but he also passed by on the other side.

"Then a despised Samaritan came along, and when he saw the man, he felt compassion for him. Going over to him, the Samaritan soothed his wounds with olive oil and wine and bandaged them. Then he put the man on his own donkey and took him to an inn, where he took care of him. The next day he handed the innkeeper two silver coins, telling him, ' Take care of this man. If his bill runs higher than this, I'll pay you the next time I'm here.'

"Now which of these three would you say was a neighbor to the man who was attacked by bandits?" Jesus asked.

The man replied, "The one who showed him mercy."

Then Jesus said, "Yes, now go and do the same."

As Jesus and the disciples continued on their way to Jerusalem, they came to a certain village

where a woman named Martha welcomed them into
her home. Her sister, Mary, sat at the Lord's feet,
listening to what he taught. But Martha was
distracted by the big dinner she was preparing. She
came to Jesus and said, "Lord, doesn't it seem unfair
to you that my sister just sits here while I do all the
work? Tell her to come and help me."

But the Lord said to her, "My dear Martha, you
are worried and upset over all these details! There is
only one thing worth being concerned about. Mary
has discovered it, and it will not be taken away from
her."

Once Jesus was in a certain place praying. As he
finished, one of his disciples came to him and said,
"Lord, teach us to pray, just as John taught his
disciples."

Jesus said, "This is how you should pray:

"Father, may your name be kept holy.
May your Kingdom come soon. Give us
each day the food we need, and forgive us
our sins, as we forgive those who sin
against us. And don't let us yield to
temptation."

Then, teaching them more about prayer, he
used this story: "Suppose you went to a friend's
house at midnight, wanting to borrow three loaves
of bread. You say to him, 'A friend of mine has just
arrived for a visit, and I have nothing for him to eat.'
And suppose he calls out from his bedroom, 'Don't
bother me. The door is locked for the night, and my
family and I are all in bed. I can't help you.' But I tell
you this—though he won't do it for friendship's
sake, if you keep knocking long enough, he will get

up and give you whatever you need because of your shameless persistence.

"And so I tell you, keep on asking, and you will receive what you ask for. Keep on seeking, and you will find. Keep on knocking, and the door will be opened to you. For everyone who asks, receives. Everyone who seeks, finds. And to everyone who knocks, the door will be opened.

"You fathers—if your children ask for a fish, do you give them a snake instead? Or if they ask for an egg, do you give them a scorpion? Of course not! So if you sinful people know how to give good gifts to your children, how much more will your heavenly Father give the Holy Spirit to those who ask him."

One day Jesus cast out a demon from a man who was blind and couldn't speak, and when the demon was gone, the man began to speak. The crowds were amazed, but some of the Pharisees and teachers of the religious law said, "He's possessed by Satan. No wonder he can cast out demons. He gets his power from Satan, the prince of demons." Others, trying to test Jesus, demanded that he show them a miraculous sign from heaven to prove his authority.

He knew their thoughts, so he said, "Any kingdom divided by civil war is doomed. A family splintered by feuding will fall apart. You say I am empowered by Satan. But if Satan is divided and fighting against himself, how can his kingdom survive? And if I am empowered by Satan, what about your own exorcists? They cast out demons, too, so they will condemn you for what you have said. But if I am casting out demons by the power of God, then the Kingdom of God has arrived among you. For when a strong man like Satan is fully armed and guards his palace, his possessions are safe—until someone even stronger attacks and overpowers him, strips him of his weapons, and carries off his belongings.

"Anyone who isn't with me opposes me, and anyone who isn't working with me is actually working against me.

"When an evil spirit leaves a person, it goes into the desert, searching for rest. But when it finds none, it says, 'I will return to the person I came from.' So it returns and finds that its former home empty, swept, and in order. Then the spirit finds seven other spirits more evil than itself, and they all enter the person and live there. And so that person is worse off than before. That will be the experience of this evil generation."

As he was speaking, a woman in the crowd called out, "God bless your mother—the womb from which you came, and the breasts that nursed you!"

Jesus replied, "But even more blessed are all who hear the word of God and put it into practice."

As the crowd pressed in on Jesus, he said, "This evil, adulterous generation keeps asking me to show them a miraculous sign. But the only sign I will give them is the sign of Jonah. What happened to him was a sign to the people of Nineveh that God had sent him. What happens to the Son of Man will be a sign to these people that he was sent by God.

"The queen of Sheba will stand up against this generation on judgment day and condemn it, for she came from a distant land to hear the wisdom of Solomon. Now someone greater than Solomon is here—but you refuse to listen. The people of

Reflection

{🧠} When you read Jesus' instructions to His followers, what comes to mind about being disciple of Jesus?

💜 What encourages you or chal-lenges you from this section?

Nineveh will also stand up against this generation on judgment day and condemn it, for they repented of their sins at the preaching of Jonah. Now someone greater than Jonah is here—but you refuse to repent.

"No one lights a lamp and then hides it or puts it under a basket. Instead, a lamp is placed on a stand, where its light can be seen by all who enter the house.

"Your eye is a lamp that provides light for your body. When your eye is good, your whole body is filled with light. But when it is bad, your body is filled with darkness. Make sure that the light you think you have is not actually darkness. If you are filled with light, with no dark corners, then your whole life will be radiant, as though a floodlight were filling you with light."

As Jesus was speaking, one of the Pharisees invited him home for a meal. So he went in and took his place at the table. His host was amazed to see that he sat down to eat without first performing the hand-washing ceremony required by Jewish custom. Then the Lord said to him, "You Pharisees are so careful to clean the outside of the cup and the dish, but inside you are filthy—full of greed and wickedness! Fools! Didn't God make the inside as well as the outside? So clean the inside by giving gifts to the poor, and you will be clean all over.

"What sorrow awaits you Pharisees! For you are careful to tithe even the tiniest income from your herb gardens, but you ignore justice and the love of

God. You should tithe, yes, but do not neglect the more important things.

"What sorrow awaits you Pharisees! For you love to sit in the seats of honor in the synagogues and receive respectful greetings as you walk in the marketplaces. Yes, what sorrow awaits you! For you are like hidden graves in a field. People walk over them without knowing the corruption they are stepping on."

"Teacher," said an expert in religious law, "you have insulted us, too, in what you just said."

"Yes," said Jesus, "what sorrow also awaits you experts in religious law! For you crush people with impossible religious demands, and you never lift a finger to ease the burden. What sorrow awaits you! For you build monuments for the prophets your own ancestors killed long ago. But in fact, you stand as witnesses who agree with what your ancestors did. They killed the prophets, and you join in their crime by building the monuments! This is what God in his wisdom said about you: 'I will send prophets and apostles to them, but they will kill some and persecute the others.'

"As a result, this generation will be held responsible for the murder of all God's prophets from the creation of the world— from the murder of Abel to the murder of Zechariah, who was killed between the altar and the sanctuary. Yes, it will certainly be charged against this generation.

"What sorrow awaits you experts in religious law! For you remove the key to knowledge from the people. You don't enter the Kingdom yourselves, and you prevent others from entering."

As Jesus was leaving, the teachers of religious law and the Pharisees became hostile and tried to provoke him with many questions. They wanted to trap him into saying something they could use against him.

Even in the face of opposition, Jesus continues to teach His disciples and the crowds using various parables. His stories provide both warnings and encouragement to all concerning the way they should live and about the future.

Meanwhile, the crowds grew until thousands were milling about and stepping on each other. Jesus turned first to his disciples and warned them, "Beware of the yeast of the Pharisees—their hypocrisy. The time is coming when everything that is covered up will be revealed, and all that is secret will be made known to all. Whatever you have said in the dark will be heard in the light, and what you have whispered behind closed doors will be shouted from the housetops for all to hear!

"Dear friends, don't be afraid of those who want to kill your body; they cannot do any more to you after that. But I'll tell you whom to fear. Fear God, who has the power to kill you and then throw you into hell. Yes, he's the one to fear.

"What is the price of five sparrows—two copper coins? Yet God does not forget a single one of them. And the very hairs on your head are all numbered. So don't be afraid; you are more valuable to God than a whole flock of sparrows.

"I tell you the truth, everyone who acknowledges me publicly here on earth, the Son of Man will also acknowledge in the presence of God's angels. But anyone who denies me here on earth will be denied before God's angels. Anyone who speaks against the Son of Man can be forgiven, but anyone who blasphemes the Holy Spirit will not be forgiven.

"And when you are brought to trial in the synagogues and before rulers and authorities, don't worry about how to defend yourself or what to say, for the Holy Spirit will teach you at that time what needs to be said."

Then someone called from the crowd, "Teacher, please tell my brother to divide our father's estate with me."

Jesus replied, "Friend, who made me a judge over you to decide such things as that?" Then he said, "Beware! Guard against every kind of greed. Life is not measured by how much you own."

Then he told them a story: "A rich man had a fertile farm that produced fine crops. He said to himself, 'What should I do? I don't have room for all my crops.' Then he said, 'I know! I'll tear down my barns and build bigger ones. Then I'll have room enough to store all my wheat and other goods. And I'll sit back and say to myself, "My friend, you have enough stored away for years to come. Now take it easy! Eat, drink, and be merry!"'

"But God said to him, 'You fool! You will die this very night. Then who will get everything you worked for?'

"Yes, a person is a fool to store up earthly wealth but not have a rich relationship with God."

Then, turning to his disciples, Jesus said, "That is why I tell you not to worry about everyday life— whether you have enough food to eat or enough clothes to wear. For life is more than food, and your body more than clothing. Look at the ravens. They don't plant or harvest or store food in barns, for God feeds them. And you are far more valuable to him than any birds! Can all your worries add a single moment to your life? And if worry can't accomplish a little thing like that, what's the use of worrying over bigger things?

"Look at the lilies and how they grow. They don't work or make their clothing, yet Solomon in all his glory was not dressed as beautifully as they are. And if God cares so wonderfully for flowers that are here today and thrown into the fire tomorrow, he will certainly care for you. Why do you have so little faith?

"And don't be concerned about what to eat and what to drink. Don't worry about such things. These things dominate the thoughts of unbelievers all over the world, but your Father already knows your needs. Seek the Kingdom of God above all else, and he will give you everything you need.

"So don't be afraid, little flock. For it gives your Father great happiness to give you the Kingdom.

"Sell your possessions and give to those in need. This will store up treasure for you in heaven! And the purses of heaven never get old or develop holes. Your treasure will be safe; no thief can steal it and no moth can destroy it. Wherever your treasure is, there the desires of your heart will also be.

"Be dressed for service and keep your lamps burning, as though you were waiting for your master to return from the wedding feast. Then you will be ready to open the door and let him in the moment he arrives and knocks. The servants who are ready and waiting for his return will be rewarded. I tell you the truth, he himself will seat them, put on an apron, and serve them as they sit and eat! He may come in the middle of the night or just before dawn. But whenever he comes, he will reward the servants who are ready.

"Understand this: If a homeowner knew exactly when a burglar was coming, he would not permit his house to be broken into. You also must be ready all the time, for the Son of Man will come when least expected."

Peter asked, "Lord, is that illustration just for us or for everyone?"

And the Lord replied, "A faithful, sensible servant is one to whom the master can give the responsibility of managing his other household servants and feeding them. If the master returns and finds that the servant has done a good job, there will be a reward. I tell you the truth, the master will put that servant in charge of all he owns. But what if the servant thinks, 'My master won't be back for a while,' and he begins beating the other servants, partying, and getting drunk? The master will return unannounced and unexpected, and he will cut the servant in pieces and banish him with the unfaithful.

"And a servant who knows what the master wants, but isn't prepared and doesn't carry out those instructions, will be severely punished. But someone who does not know, and then does something wrong, will be punished only lightly. When someone has been given much, much will be required in return; and when someone has been entrusted with much, even more will be required.

"I have come to set the world on fire, and I wish it were already burning! I have a terrible baptism of suffering ahead of me, and I am under a

Reflection

What does Jesus teach about living a faith filled life? What illustrations where helpful to you?

Once again Jesus describes the cost of discipleship. How does that impact you and your life today?

heavy burden until it is accomplished. Do you think I have come to bring peace to the earth? No, I have come to divide people against each other! From now on families will be split apart, three in favor of me, and two against—or two in favor and three against.

'Father will be divided against son and son against father; mother against daughter and daughter against mother; and mother-in-law against daughter-in-law and daughter-in-law against mother-in-law.' "

Then Jesus turned to the crowd and said, "When you see clouds beginning to form in the west, you say, 'Here comes a shower.' And you are right. When the south wind blows, you say, ' Today will be a scorcher.' And it is. You fools! You know how to interpret the weather signs of the earth and sky, but you don't know how to interpret the present times.

"Why can't you decide for yourselves what is right? When you are on the way to court with your accuser, try to settle the matter before you get there. Otherwise, your accuser may drag you before the judge, who will hand you over to an officer, who will throw you into prison. And if that happens, you won't be free again until you have paid the very last penny."

About this time Jesus was informed that Pilate had murdered some people from Galilee as they were offering sacrifices at the Temple. "Do you think those Galileans were worse sinners than all the other people from Galilee?" Jesus asked. "Is that why they suffered? Not at all! And you will perish, too, unless you repent of your sins and turn to God. And what about the eighteen people who died when the tower in Siloam fell on them? Were they the worst sinners in Jerusalem? No, and I tell you again that unless you repent, you will perish, too."

Then Jesus told this story: "A man planted a fig tree in his garden and came again and again to see if there was any fruit on it, but he was always disappointed. Finally, he said to his gardener, 'I've waited three years, and there hasn't been a single fig! Cut it down. It's just taking up space in the garden.'

"The gardener answered, 'Sir, give it one more chance. Leave it another year, and I'll give it special attention and plenty of fertilizer. If we get figs next year, fine. If not, then you can cut it down.' "

One Sabbath day as Jesus was teaching in a synagogue, he saw a woman who had been crippled by an evil spirit. She had been bent double for eighteen years and was unable to stand up straight. When Jesus saw her, he called her over and said, "Dear woman, you are healed of your sickness!" Then he touched her, and instantly she could stand straight. How she praised God!

But the leader in charge of the synagogue was indignant that Jesus had healed her on the Sabbath day. "There are six days of the week for working," he said to the crowd. "Come on those days to be healed, not on the Sabbath."

But the Lord replied, "You hypocrites! Each of you works on the Sabbath day! Don't you untie your ox or your donkey from its stall on the Sabbath and lead it out for water? This dear woman, a daughter of Abraham, has been held in bondage by Satan for

eighteen years. Isn't it right that she be released, even
on the Sabbath?"

This shamed his enemies, but all the people
rejoiced at the wonderful things he did.

Then Jesus said, "What is the Kingdom of God
like? How can I illustrate it? It is like a tiny mustard
seed that a man planted in a garden; it grows and
becomes a tree, and the birds make nests in its
branches."

He also asked, "What else is the Kingdom of
God like? It is like the yeast a woman used in
making bread. Even though she put only a little yeast
in three measures of flour, it permeated every part of
the dough."

> *After Jesus heals once again on the Sabbath, it is*
> *now time for The Festival of Dedication, or*
> *Hanukkah. This particular festival follows the*
> *Festival of Shelters on the Jewish calendar and*
> *commemorates the rededication of the Temple in*
> *165 B.C. Unlike the three major festivals, The*
> *Festival of Dedication is not instituted by Jewish*
> *Scriptures, so it is not a required pilgrimage.*
> *However, no one could deny that the eight-day*
> *celebration of lights in the Temple was beautiful.*
> *Many pious Jews from nearby Galilee would come*
> *to Jerusalem to celebrate. Unfortunately, such a*
> *beautiful celebration does not subdue the*
> *increasing rage the Pharisees have toward Jesus'*
> *powerful teaching.*

It was now winter, and Jesus was in Jerusalem
at the time of Hanukkah, the Festival of Dedication.
He was in the Temple, walking through the section
known as Solomon's Colonnade. The people
surrounded him and asked, "How long are you

going to keep us in suspense? If you are the Messiah, tell us plainly."

Jesus replied, "I have already told you, and you don't believe me. The proof is the work I do in my Father's name. But you don't believe me because you are not my sheep. My sheep listen to my voice; I know them, and they follow me. I give them eternal life, and they will never perish. No one can snatch them away from me, for my Father has given them to me, and he is more powerful than anyone else. No one can snatch them from the Father's hand. The Father and I are one."

Once again the people picked up stones to kill him. Jesus said, "At my Father's direction I have done many good works. For which one are you going to stone me?"

They replied, "We're stoning you not for any good work, but for blasphemy! You, a mere man, claim to be God."

Jesus replied, "It is written in your own Scriptures that God said to certain leaders of the people, 'I say, you are gods!' And you know that the Scriptures cannot be altered. So if those people who received God's message were called 'gods,' why do you call it blasphemy when I say, 'I am the Son of God'? After all, the Father set me apart and sent me into the world. Don't believe me unless I carry out my Father's work. But if I do his work, believe in the evidence of the miraculous works I have done, even if you don't believe me. Then you will know and understand that the Father is in me, and I am in the Father."

Once again they tried to arrest him, but he got away and left them. He went beyond the Jordan

River near the place where John was first baptizing and stayed there awhile. And many followed him. "John didn't perform miraculous signs," they remarked to one another, "but everything he said about this man has come true." And many who were there believed in Jesus.

Jesus went through the towns and villages, teaching as he went, always pressing on toward Jerusalem. Someone asked him, "Lord, will only a few be saved?"

He replied, "Work hard to enter the narrow door to God's Kingdom, for many will try to enter but will fail. When the master of the house has locked the door, it will be too late. You will stand outside knocking and pleading, 'Lord, open the door for us!' But he will reply, 'I don't know you or where you come from.' Then you will say, 'But we ate and drank with you, and you taught in our streets.' And he will reply, 'I tell you, I don't know you or where you come from. Get away from me, all you who do evil.'

"There will be weeping and gnashing of teeth, for you will see Abraham, Isaac, Jacob, and all the prophets in the Kingdom of God, but you will be thrown out. And people will come from all over the world—from east and west, north and south—to take their places in the Kingdom of God. And note this: Some who seem least important now will be the greatest then, and some who are the greatest now will be least important then."

At that time some Pharisees said to him, "Get away from here if you want to live! Herod Antipas wants to kill you!"

Jesus replied, "Go tell that fox that I will keep on casting out demons and healing people today and tomorrow; and the third day I will accomplish my purpose. Yes, today, tomorrow, and the next day I must proceed on my way. For it wouldn't do for a prophet of God to be killed except in Jerusalem!

"O Jerusalem, Jerusalem, the city that kills the prophets and stones God's messengers! How often I have wanted to gather your children together as a hen protects her chicks beneath her wings, but you wouldn't let me. And now, look, your house is abandoned. And you will never see me again until you say, 'Blessings on the one who comes in the name of the LORD!' "

One Sabbath day Jesus went to eat dinner in the home of a leader of the Pharisees, and the people were watching him closely. There was a man there whose arms and legs were swollen. Jesus asked the Pharisees and experts in religious law, "Is it permitted in the law to heal people on the Sabbath day, or not?" When they refused to answer, Jesus touched the sick man and healed him and sent him away. Then he turned to them and said, "Which of you doesn't work on the Sabbath? If your son or your cow falls into a pit, don't you rush to get him out?" Again they could not answer.

When Jesus noticed that all who had come to the dinner were trying to sit in the seats of honor near the head of the table, he gave them this advice: "When you are invited to a wedding feast, don't sit in the seat of honor. What if someone who is more distinguished than you has also been invited? The host will come and say, 'Give this person your seat.' Then you will be embarrassed, and you will have to take whatever seat is left at the foot of the table!

"Instead, take the lowest place at the foot of the table. Then when your host sees you, he will come and say, 'Friend, we have a better place for you!' Then you will be honored in front of all the other guests. For those who exalt themselves will be humbled, and those who humble themselves will be exalted."

Then he turned to his host. "When you put on a luncheon or a banquet," he said, "don't invite your friends, brothers, relatives, and rich neighbors. For they will invite you back, and that will be your only reward. Instead, invite the poor, the crippled, the lame, and the blind. Then at the resurrection of the righteous, God will reward you for inviting those who could not repay you."

Hearing this, a man sitting at the table with Jesus exclaimed, "What a blessing it will be to attend a banquet in the Kingdom of God!"

Jesus replied with this story: "A man prepared a great feast and sent out many invitations. When the banquet was ready, he sent his servant to tell the guests, 'Come, the banquet is ready.' But they all began making excuses. One said, 'I have just bought a field and must inspect it. Please excuse me.' Another said, 'I have just bought five pairs of oxen, and I want to try them out. Please excuse me.' Another said, 'I now have a wife, so I can't come.'

"The servant returned and told his master what they had said. His master was furious and said, 'Go quickly into the streets and alleys of the town and invite the poor, the crippled, the blind, and the lame.' After the servant had done this, he reported, 'There is still room for more.' So his master said, 'Go out into the country lanes and behind the hedges and urge anyone you find to come, so that

the house will be full. For none of those I first
invited will get even the smallest taste of my
banquet.' "

*It's been said that if you're not offending anyone
you're probably doing something wrong. If that's
true, Jesus must be doing everything right. He
directly challenges the teaching of the Jewish
leaders in the Temple courts and insults them in
almost every encounter. He takes it a step further
by protecting and even forgiving an adulterous
woman, who according to Jewish law should be
stoned (capital punishment in that time). The
religious authorities are still upset that Jesus heals
and drives out demons, even on the Sabbath. And
worst of all, He teaches with divine authority and
even claims to be God! Sensing danger, it's time
for Jesus to leave Jerusalem, but He'll be back
soon enough.*

Scripture References

John 7:11—10:42; Matthew 8:19–22,
12:22–45; Luke 9:57—14:24; Mark 3:20–
30

Reflection

Jesus
speaks   much
about   the
kingdom   of
God.   What
stands out to
you about the
Kingdom   of
God?

Think of
a time when
you   invited
people to join
you for a meal
or celebration.
How did that
make you feel?

Chapter 9

Jesus Teaches About True Discipleship

After leaving Jerusalem, Jesus returns to safety across the Jordan River to Perea where John the Baptist ministered. He still has a large group of admirers, but many have also abandoned Him. But it's no time for Jesus to back off. He will now elaborate even more about a tough but necessary topic—the cost of true discipleship.

A large crowd was following Jesus. He turned around and said to them, "If you want to be my disciple, you must hate everyone else by comparison—your father and mother, wife and children, brothers and sisters—yes, even your own life. Otherwise, you cannot be my disciple. And if you do not carry your own cross and follow me, you cannot be my disciple.

"But don't begin until you count the cost. For who would begin construction of a building without first calculating the cost to see if there is enough money to finish it? Otherwise, you might complete only the foundation before running out of money, and then everyone would laugh at you. They would say, ' There's the person who started that building and couldn't afford to finish it!'

"Or what king would go to war against another king without first sitting down with his counselors to discuss whether his army of 10,000 could defeat the 20,000 soldiers marching against him? And if he can't, he will send a delegation to discuss terms of peace while the enemy is still far away. So you cannot become my disciple without giving up everything you own.

"Salt is good for seasoning. But if it loses its flavor, how do you make it salty again? Flavorless salt is good neither for the soil nor for the manure pile. It is thrown away. Anyone with ears to hear should listen and understand!"

Tax collectors and other notorious sinners often came to listen to Jesus teach. This made the Pharisees and teachers of religious law complain that he was associating with such sinful people—even eating with them!

So Jesus told them this story: "If a man has a hundred sheep and one of them gets lost, what will he do? Won't he leave the ninety-nine others in the wilderness and go to search for the one that is lost until he finds it? And when he has found it, he will joyfully carry it home on his shoulders. When he arrives, he will call together his friends and neighbors, saying, 'Rejoice with me because I have found my lost sheep.' In the same way, there is more joy in heaven over one lost sinner who repents and returns to God than over ninety-nine others who are righteous and haven't strayed away!

"Or suppose a woman has ten silver coins and loses one. Won't she light a lamp and sweep the entire house and search carefully until she finds it? And when she finds it, she will call in her friends and neighbors and say, 'Rejoice with me because I have found my lost coin.' In the same way, there is joy in the presence of God's angels when even one sinner repents."

To illustrate the point further, Jesus told them this story: "A man had two sons. The younger son told his father, 'I want my share of your estate now before you die.' So his father agreed to divide his wealth between his sons.

"A few days later this younger son packed all his belongings and moved to a distant land, and there he wasted all his money in wild living. About the time his money ran out, a great famine swept over the land, and he began to starve. He persuaded a local farmer to hire him, and the man sent him into his fields to feed the pigs. The young man became so hungry that even the pods he was feeding the pigs looked good to him. But no one gave him anything.

"When he finally came to his senses, he said to himself, 'At home even the hired servants have food enough to spare, and here I am dying of hunger! I will go home to my father and say, "Father, I have sinned against both heaven and you, and I am no longer worthy of being called your son. Please take me on as a hired servant."'

"So he returned home to his father. And while he was still a long way off, his father saw him coming. Filled with love and compassion, he ran to his son, embraced him, and kissed him. His son said to him, 'Father, I have sinned against both heaven and you, and I am no longer worthy of being called your son.'

"But his father said to the servants, 'Quick! Bring the finest robe in the house and put it on him. Get a ring for his finger and sandals for his feet. And kill the calf we have been fattening. We must celebrate with a feast, for this son of mine was dead and has now returned to life. He was lost, but now he is found.' So the party began.

"Meanwhile, the older son was in the fields working. When he returned home, he heard music and dancing in the house, and he asked one of the servants what was going on. ' Your brother is back,' he was told, 'and your father has killed the fattened calf. We are celebrating because of his safe return.'

"The older brother was angry and wouldn't go in. His father came out and begged him, but he replied, 'All these years I've slaved for you and never once refused to do a single thing you told me to. And in all that time you never gave me even one young goat for a feast with my friends. Yet when this son of yours comes back after squandering your money on prostitutes, you celebrate by killing the fattened calf!'

"His father said to him, 'Look, dear son, you have always stayed by me, and everything I have is yours. We had to celebrate this happy day. For your brother was dead and has come back to life! He was lost, but now he is found!' "

Jesus surrounds Himself with notorious sinners and corrupt tax collectors that the people despise. Predictably, this draws a fair amount of criticism from the Pharisees. But as Jesus said before, it's not the healthy that need a doctor. Jesus diagnoses the Pharisees' true problem as greed. He then uses two parables to paint a picture that illustrates both the proper use of money and the insidious dangers of loving money too much.

Jesus told this story to his disciples: "There was a certain rich man who had a manager handling his affairs. One day a report came that the manager was wasting his employer's money. So the employer called him in and said, 'What's this I hear about you?

Get your report in order, because you are going to be fired.'

"The manager thought to himself, 'Now what? My boss has fired me. I don't have the strength to dig ditches, and I'm too proud to beg. Ah, I know how to ensure that I'll have plenty of friends who will give me a home when I am fired.'

"So he invited each person who owed money to his employer to come and discuss the situation. He asked the first one, 'How much do you owe him?' The man replied, 'I owe him 800 gallons of olive oil.' So the manager told him, 'Take the bill and quickly change it to 400 gallons.'

" 'And how much do you owe my employer?' he asked the next man. 'I owe him 1,000 bushels of wheat,' was the reply. 'Here,' the manager said, 'take the bill and change it to 800 bushels.'

"The rich man had to admire the dishonest rascal for being so shrewd. And it is true that the children of this world are more shrewd in dealing with the world around them than are the children of the light. Here's the lesson: Use your worldly resources to benefit others and make friends. Then, when your earthly possessions are gone, they will welcome you to an eternal home.

"If you are faithful in little things, you will be faithful in large ones. But if you are dishonest in little things, you won't be honest with greater responsibilities. And if you are untrustworthy about worldly wealth, who will trust you with the true riches of heaven? And if you are not faithful with other people's things, why should you be trusted with things of your own?

"No one can serve two masters. For you will hate one and love the other; you will be devoted to one and despise the other. You cannot serve both God and money."

The Pharisees, who dearly loved their money, heard all this and scoffed at him. Then he said to them, "You like to appear righteous in public, but God knows your hearts. What this world honors is detestable in the sight of God.

"Until John the Baptist, the law of Moses and the messages of the prophets were your guides. But now the Good News of the Kingdom of God is preached, and everyone is eager to get in. But that doesn't mean that the law has lost its force. It is easier for heaven and earth to disappear than for the smallest point of God's law to be overturned.

"For example, a man who divorces his wife and marries someone else commits adultery. And anyone who marries a woman divorced from her husband commits adultery."

Jesus said, "There was a certain rich man who was splendidly clothed in purple and fine linen and who lived each day in luxury. At his gate lay a poor man named Lazarus who was covered with sores. As Lazarus lay there longing for scraps from the rich man's table, the dogs would come and lick his open sores.

"Finally, the poor man died and was carried by the angels to be with Abraham. The rich man also died and was buried, and his soul went to the place of the dead. There, in torment, he saw Abraham in the far distance with Lazarus at his side.

"The rich man shouted, ' Father Abraham, have some pity! Send Lazarus over here to dip the tip of his finger in water and cool my tongue. I am in anguish in these flames.'

"But Abraham said to him, 'Son, remember that during your lifetime you had everything you wanted, and Lazarus had nothing. So now he is here being comforted, and you are in anguish. And besides, there is a great chasm separating us. No one can cross over to you from here, and no one can cross over to us from there.'

"Then the rich man said, 'Please, Father Abraham, at least send him to my father's home. For I have five brothers, and I want him to warn them so they don't end up in this place of torment.'

Reflection

(*) What is it that causes much rejoicing in heaven?

(*) Who do you relate to in the story of the lost son? With whom can you share this story?

"But Abraham said, 'Moses and the prophets have warned them. Your brothers can read what they wrote.'

"The rich man replied, 'No, Father Abraham! But if someone is sent to them from the dead, then they will repent of their sins and turn to God.'

"But Abraham said, 'If they won't listen to Moses and the prophets, they won't listen even if someone rises from the dead.' "

⟨⟩

One day Jesus said to his disciples, "There will always be temptations to sin, but what sorrow awaits the person who does the tempting! It would be better to be thrown into the sea with a millstone hung around your neck than to cause one of these little ones to fall into sin. So watch yourselves!

"If another believer sins, rebuke that person; then if there is repentance, forgive. Even if that person wrongs you seven times a day and each time turns again and asks forgiveness, you must forgive."

The apostles said to the Lord, "Show us how to increase our faith."

The Lord answered, "If you had faith even as small as a mustard seed, you could say to this mulberry tree, 'May you be uprooted and thrown into the sea,' and it would obey you! "When a servant comes in from plowing or taking care of sheep, does his master say, 'Come in and eat with me'? No, he says, 'Prepare my meal, put on your apron, and serve me while I eat. Then you can eat later.' And does the master thank the servant for doing what he was told to do? Of course not. In the same way, when you obey me you should say, 'We are unworthy servants who have simply done our duty.' "

After He's finished teaching, Jesus receives word that His friend Lazarus is sick. By the time Jesus arrives, it's already too late; Lazarus has died. This gives Jesus a perfect opportunity to reveal His iden-tity as both man and God. As man, His compas-sion is stirring; as God, His power is incredible!

A man named Lazarus was sick. He lived in Bethany with his sisters, Mary and Martha. This is the Mary who later poured the expensive perfume on the Lord's feet and wiped them with her hair. Her brother, Lazarus, was sick. So the two sisters sent a message to Jesus telling him, "Lord, your dear friend is very sick."

But when Jesus heard about it he said, "Lazarus's sickness will not end in death. No, it happened for the glory of God so that the Son of

God will receive glory from this." So although Jesus loved Martha, Mary, and Lazarus, he stayed where he was for the next two days. Finally, he said to his disciples, "Let's go back to Judea."

But his disciples objected. "Rabbi," they said, "only a few days ago the people in Judea were trying to stone you. Are you going there again?"

Jesus replied, "There are twelve hours of daylight every day. During the day people can walk safely. They can see because they have the light of this world. But at night there is danger of stumbling because they have no light." Then he said, "Our friend Lazarus has fallen asleep, but now I will go and wake him up."

The disciples said, "Lord, if he is sleeping, he will soon get better!" They thought Jesus meant Lazarus was simply sleeping, but Jesus meant Lazarus had died.

So he told them plainly, "Lazarus is dead. And for your sakes, I'm glad I wasn't there, for now you will really believe. Come, let's go see him."

Thomas, nicknamed the Twin, said to his fellow disciples, "Let's go, too—and die with Jesus."

When Jesus arrived at Bethany, he was told that Lazarus had already been in his grave for four days. Bethany was only a few miles down the road from Jerusalem, and many of the people had come to console Martha and Mary in their loss. When Martha got word that Jesus was coming, she went to meet him. But Mary stayed in the house. Martha said to Jesus, "Lord, if only you had been here, my brother would not have died. But even now I know that God will give you whatever you ask."

Jesus told her, "Your brother will rise again."

"Yes," Martha said, "he will rise when everyone else rises, at the last day."

Jesus told her, "I am the resurrection and the life. Anyone who believes in me will live, even after dying. Everyone who lives in me and believes in me will never ever die. Do you believe this, Martha?"

"Yes, Lord," she told him. "I have always believed you are the Messiah, the Son of God, the one who has come into the world from God." Then she returned to Mary. She called Mary aside from the mourners and told her, "The Teacher is here and wants to see you." So Mary immediately went to him.

Jesus had stayed outside the village, at the place where Martha met him. When the people who were at the house consoling Mary saw her leave so hastily, they assumed she was going to Lazarus's grave to weep. So they followed her there. When Mary arrived and saw Jesus, she fell at his feet and said, "Lord, if only you had been here, my brother would not have died."

When Jesus saw her weeping and saw the other people wailing with her, a deep anger welled up within him, and he was deeply troubled. "Where have you put him?" he asked them.

They told him, "Lord, come and see." Then Jesus wept. The people who were standing nearby said, "See how much he loved him!" But some said, "This man healed a blind man. Couldn't he have kept Lazarus from dying?"

Jesus was still angry as he arrived at the tomb, a cave with a stone rolled across its entrance. "Roll the stone aside," Jesus told them.

But Martha, the dead man's sister, protested, "Lord, he has been dead for four days. The smell will be terrible."

Jesus responded, "Didn't I tell you that you would see God's glory if you believe?" So they rolled the stone aside. Then Jesus looked up to heaven and said, "Father, thank you for hearing me. You always hear me, but I said it out loud for the sake of all these people standing here, so that they will believe you sent me." Then Jesus shouted, "Lazarus, come out!" And the dead man came out, his hands and feet bound in graveclothes, his face wrapped in a headcloth. Jesus told them, "Unwrap him and let him go!"

Many of the people who were with Mary believed in Jesus when they saw this happen. But some went to the Pharisees and told them what Jesus had done. Then the leading priests and Pharisees called the high council together. "What are we going to do?" they asked each other. "This man certainly performs many miraculous signs. If we allow him to go on like this, soon everyone will believe in him. Then the Roman army will come and destroy both our Temple and our nation."

Caiaphas, who was high priest at that time, said, "You don't know what you're talking about! You don't realize that it's better for you that one man should die for the people than for the whole nation to be destroyed."

He did not say this on his own; as high priest at that time he was led to prophesy that Jesus would die for the entire nation. And not only for that nation, but to bring together and unite all the children of God scattered around the world.

So from that time on, the Jewish leaders began
to plot Jesus' death. As a result, Jesus stopped his
public ministry among the people and left
Jerusalem. He went to a place near the wilderness,
to the village of Ephraim, and stayed there with his
disciples.

*Lazarus's resurrection gives the religious leaders
the urgency they need to plan Jesus' death with a
new determination. Knowing their plans, Jesus
will now avoid Jerusalem until it's time for His
death. Regardless, He continues to perform
miracles as He travels off the beaten path. As
Jesus continued on toward Jerusalem, he reached
the border between Galilee and Samaria. As he
entered a village there, ten lepers stood at a
distance, crying out, "Jesus, Master, have mercy
on us!"*

He looked at them and said, "Go show
yourselves to the priests." And as they went, they
were cleansed of their leprosy.

One of them, when he saw that he was healed,
came back to Jesus, shouting, "Praise God!" He fell
to the ground at Jesus' feet, thanking him for what
he had done. This man was a Samaritan.

Jesus asked, "Didn't I heal ten men? Where are
the other nine? Has no one returned to give glory to
God except this foreigner?" And Jesus said to the
man, "Stand up and go. Your faith has healed you."

One day the Pharisees asked Jesus, "When will
the Kingdom of God come?"

Jesus replied, "The Kingdom of God can't be detected by visible signs. You won't be able to say, 'Here it is!' or 'It's over there!' For the Kingdom of God is already among you."

Then he said to his disciples, "The time is coming when you will long to see the day when the Son of Man returns, but you won't see it. People will tell you, 'Look, there is the Son of Man,' or 'Here he is,' but don't go out and follow them. For as the lightning flashes and lights up the sky from one end to the other, so it will be on the day when the Son of Man comes. But first the Son of Man must suffer terribly and be rejected by this generation.

"When the Son of Man returns, it will be like it was in Noah's day. In those days, the people enjoyed banquets and parties and weddings right up to the time Noah entered his boat and the flood came and destroyed them all.

"And the world will be as it was in the days of Lot. People went about their daily business—eating and drinking, buying and selling, farming and building—until the morning Lot left Sodom. Then fire and burning sulfur rained down from heaven and destroyed them all. Yes, it will be 'business as usual' right up to the day when the Son of Man is revealed. On that day a person out on the deck of a roof must not go down into the house to pack. A person out in the field must not return home. Remember what happened to Lot's wife! If you cling to your life, you will lose it, and if you let your life go, you will save it. That night two people will be asleep in one bed; one will be taken, the other left. Two women will be grinding flour together at the mill; one will be taken, the other left."

"Where will this happen, Lord?" the disciples asked.

Jesus replied, "Just as the gathering of vultures shows there is a carcass nearby, so these signs indicate that the end is near."

One day Jesus told his disciples a story to show that they should always pray and never give up. "There was a judge in a certain city," he said, "who neither feared God nor cared about people. A widow of that city came to him repeatedly, saying, 'Give me justice in this dispute with my enemy.' The judge ignored her for a while, but finally he said to himself, 'I don't fear God or care about people, but this woman is driving me crazy. I'm going to see that she gets justice, because she is wearing me out with her constant requests!' "

Then the Lord said, "Learn a lesson from this unjust judge. Even he rendered a just decision in the end. So don't you think God will surely give justice to his chosen people who cry out to him day and night? Will he keep putting them off? I tell you, he will grant justice to them quickly! But when the Son of Man returns, how many will he find on the earth who have faith?"

Then Jesus told this story to some who had great confidence in their own righteousness and scorned everyone else: "Two men went to the Temple to pray. One was a Pharisee, and the other was a despised tax collector. The Pharisee stood by himself and prayed this prayer: 'I thank you, God, that I am not a sinner like everyone else. For I don't cheat, I don't sin, and I don't commit adultery. I'm certainly not like that tax collector! I fast twice a week, and I give you a tenth of my income.'

"But the tax collector stood at a distance and dared not even lift his eyes to heaven as he prayed. Instead, he beat his chest in sorrow, saying, 'O God, be merciful to me, for I am a sinner.' I tell you, this sinner, not the Pharisee, returned home justified before God. For those who exalt themselves will be humbled, and those who humble themselves will be exalted."

When Jesus had finished saying these things, he left Galilee and went down to the region of Judea east of the Jordan River. Once again, large crowds followed him there, and as usual he was teaching them and healed their sick.

Some Pharisees came and tried to trap him with this question: "Should a man be allowed to divorce his wife for just any reason?" "Haven't you read the Scriptures?" Jesus replied. "They record that from the beginning 'God made them male and female.' And he said, 'This explains why a man leaves his father and mother and is joined to his wife, and the two are united into one.' Since they are no longer two but one, let no one split apart what God has joined together."

"Then why did Moses say in the law that a man could give his wife a written notice of divorce and send her away?" they asked.

Jesus replied, "Moses permitted divorce only as a concession to your hard hearts, but it was not what God had originally intended. And I tell you this, whoever divorces his wife and marries someone else commits adultery against her—unless his wife has been unfaithful. And if a woman divorces her husband and marries someone else, she commits adultery. And anyone who marries a woman divorced from her husband commits adultery."

Later, when he was alone with his disciples in the house, Jesus' disciples then said to him, "If this is the case, it is better not to marry!"

"Not everyone can accept this statement," Jesus said. "Only those whom God helps. Some are born as eunuchs, some have been made eunuchs by others, and some choose not to marry for the sake of the Kingdom of Heaven. Let anyone accept this who can."

Reflection

What does Jesus teach about prayer?

Reflect on the role prayer is playing in your life. What are you asking, seeking, knocking for?

Jesus just finished teaching about divorce and prayer, yet His disciples still struggle to understand. Jesus rebukes them again and continues to patiently teach about the Kingdom of God.

One day some parents brought their children to Jesus so he could touch and bless them. But the disciples scolded the parents for bothering him.

When Jesus saw what was happening, he was angry with his disciples. Then Jesus called for the children and said to them, "Let the children come to me. Don't stop them! For the Kingdom of God belongs to those who are like these children. I tell you the truth, anyone who doesn't receive the Kingdom of God like a child will never enter it." Then he took the children in his arms and placed his hands on their heads and blessed them before he left.

As Jesus was starting out on his way to Jerusalem, a man came running up to him, knelt down, and asked, "Good Teacher, what good deed must I do to inherit eternal life?"

"Why do you call me good?" Jesus asked. "Only God is truly good. But to answer your question—keep the commandments."

"Which ones?" the man asked.

And Jesus replied: "You know the commandments: 'You must not murder. You must not commit adultery. You must not steal. You must not testify falsely. You must not cheat anyone. Honor your father and mother. Love your neighbor as yourself.'"

"Teacher," the young man replied, "I've obeyed all these commandments since I was young. What else must I do?"

Looking at the man, Jesus felt genuine love for him. "There is still one thing you haven't done," he told him. "Go and sell all your possessions and give the money to the poor, and you will have treasure in heaven. Then come, follow me."

At this the man's face fell, and he went away very sad, for he had many possessions.

Jesus looked around and said to his disciples, "How hard it is for the rich to enter the Kingdom of God!" This amazed them. But Jesus said again, "Dear children, it is very hard to enter the Kingdom of God. In fact, it is easier for a camel to go through the eye of a needle than for a rich person to enter the Kingdom of God!"

The disciples were astounded. "Then who in the world can be saved?" they asked.

Jesus looked at them intently and said, "Humanly speaking, it is impossible. But not with God. Every-thing is possible with God."

Then Peter began to speak up. "We've given up everything to follow you," he said.

"Yes," Jesus replied, "and I assure you that when the world is made new and the Son of Man sits upon his glorious throne, you who have been my followers will also sit on twelve thrones, judging the twelve tribes of Israel. I assure you that everyone who has given up house or wife or brothers or sisters or mother or father or children or property, for my sake and for the Good News, will receive now in return a hundred times as many houses, brothers, sisters, mothers, children, and property— along with persecution. And in the world to come that person will have eternal life. But many who are the greatest now will be least important then, and those who seem least important now will be the greatest then."

"For the Kingdom of Heaven is like the landowner who went out early one morning to hire workers for his vineyard. He agreed to pay the normal daily wage and sent them out to work.

"At nine o'clock in the morning he was passing through the marketplace and saw some people standing around doing nothing. So he hired them, telling them he would pay them whatever was right at the end of the day. So they went to work in the vineyard. At noon and again at three o'clock he did the same thing.

"At five o'clock that afternoon he was in town again and saw some more people standing around. He asked them, 'Why haven't you been working today?'

"They replied, 'Because no one hired us.'

"The landowner told them, ' Then go out and join the others in my vineyard.'

"That evening he told the foreman to call the workers in and pay them, beginning with the last workers first. When those hired at five o'clock were paid, each received a full day's wage. When those hired first came to get their pay, they assumed they would receive more. But they, too, were paid a day's wage. When they received their pay, they protested to the owner, ' Those people worked only one hour, and yet you've paid them just as much as you paid us who worked all day in the scorching heat.'

"He answered one of them, 'Friend, I haven't been unfair! Didn't you agree to work all day for the usual wage? Take your money and go. I wanted to pay this last worker the same as you. Is it against the law for me to do what I want with my money? Should you be jealous because I am kind to others?'

"So those who are last now will be first then, and those who are first will be last."

It is time! Jesus and the disciples head to Jerusalem for His final visit. As they travel, Jesus predicts His death and resurrection for the third time. Jesus continues to perform miracles and befriend sinners and tax collectors. Though His disciples are still confused by Jesus' teaching, they are also unwavering in their loyalty to their Lord.

They were now on the way up to Jerusalem, and Jesus was walking ahead of them. The disciples were filled with awe, and the people following behind were overwhelmed with fear. Taking the twelve disciples aside, Jesus once more began to describe everything that was about to happen to him. "Listen," he said, "we're going up to Jerusalem, where all the predictions of the prophets concerning the Son of Man will come true. The Son of Man will be betrayed to the leading priests and the teachers of religious law. They will sentence him to die and hand him over to the Romans. They will mock him, spit on him, flog him with a whip, and kill him, but after three days he will rise again."

Then the mother of James and John, the sons of Zebedee, came over to Jesus with her sons and they spoke to him. "Teacher," they said, "we want you to do us a favor."

"What is your request?" he asked.

They replied, "When you sit on your glorious throne, we want to sit in places of honor next to you, one on your right and the other on your left."

But Jesus said to them, "You don't know what you are asking! Are you able to drink from the bitter cup of suffering I am about to drink? Are you able to be baptized with the baptism of suffering I must be baptized with?"

"Oh yes," they replied, "we are able!"

Then Jesus told them, "You will indeed drink from my bitter cup and be baptized with my baptism of suffering. But I have no right to say who will sit on my right or my left. My Father has prepared those places for the ones he has chosen."

When the ten other disciples heard what James and John had asked, they were indignant. So Jesus called them together and said, "You know that the rulers in this world lord it over their people, and officials flaunt their authority over those under them. But among you it will be different. Whoever wants to be a leader among you must be your servant, and whoever wants to be first among you must be the slave of everyone else. For even the Son of Man came not to be served but to serve others and to give his life as a ransom for many."

Then they reached Jericho, and as Jesus and his disciples left town, a large crowd followed him. A blind beggar named Bartimaeus (son of Timaeus)[30] was sitting beside the road.

When he heard the noise of a crowd going past, he asked what was happening. They told him that Jesus the Nazarene was going by. So he began shouting, "Jesus, Son of David, have mercy on me!"

"Be quiet!" the people in front yelled at him.

But he only shouted louder, "Son of David, have mercy on me!"

When Jesus heard him, he stopped and said, "Tell him to come here." So they called the blind man. "Cheer up," they said. "Come on, he's calling you!" Bartimaeus threw aside his coat, jumped up, and came to Jesus.

"What do you want me to do for you?" Jesus asked.

"Lord," the blind man said, "I want to see!"

And Jesus said to him, "Go, for your faith has healed you."[31]

Instantly the man could see, and he followed Jesus, praising God. And all who saw it praised God, too.

---

[30] Similar to the story of the demon-possessed man on page 92, Matthew reports that there are two blind men while both Mark and Luke only mention one man, Bartimaeus. Mark and Luke simply choose to feature the one who did the speaking, Bartimaeus, the more prominent of the two.

[31] Matthew tells us that Jesus "felt sorry for them and touched their eyes."

Reflection

Jesus entered Jericho and made his way through the town. There was a man there named Zacchaeus. He was the chief tax collector[32] in the region, and he had become very rich. He tried to get a look at Jesus, but he was too short to see over the crowd. So he ran ahead and climbed a sycamore-fig tree beside the road, for Jesus was going to pass that way.

When Jesus came by, he looked up at Zacchaeus and called him by name. "Zacchaeus!" he said. "Quick, come down! I must be a guest in your home today."

Zacchaeus quickly climbed down and took Jesus to his house in great excitement and joy. But the people were displeased. "He has gone to be the guest of a notorious sinner," they grumbled.

Meanwhile, Zacchaeus stood before the Lord and said, "I will give half my wealth to the poor,

How does Jesus respond to the question "What must I do to be saved?

Who in your relationships most exemplifies a servant leader as Jesus described? Consider sharing that with them.

---

[32] **chief tax collector**: In the Jewish Mishnah (Oral Law), tax collectors were considered subhuman. For example, it was forbidden to lie unless it was to a tax collector because it was the same as lying to a dog. Understanding the context helps to explain this extreme reaction. Israel was one of many states conquered by Rome. In order to hide as much taxable income as possible, the merchants of these conquered states would operate underground and in black markets. Rome's counter-measure was to hire a local person who knew where the money was to be a tax collector. Rome would also issue a company of soldiers who would accompany the tax collectors as they collected. In addition, Rome didn't care how much these tax collectors collected as long as they received their share. So these tax collectors got very rich by turning in their friends, neighbors, and fellow countrymen to the conquering power and robbing them of hard-earned money by over-taxing in order to line their own pockets.

Lord, and if I have cheated people on their taxes, I will give them back four times as much!"

Jesus responded, "Salvation has come to this home today, for this man has shown himself to be a true son of Abraham. For the Son of Man came to seek and save those who are lost."

The crowd was listening to everything Jesus said. And because he was nearing Jerusalem, he told them a story to correct the impression that the Kingdom of God would begin right away. He said, "A nobleman was called away to a distant empire to be crowned king and then return. Before he left, he called together ten of his servants and divided among them ten pounds of silver, saying, 'Invest this for me while I am gone.' But his people hated him and sent a delegation after him to say, 'We do not want him to be our king.'

"After he was crowned king, he returned and called in the servants to whom he had given the money. He wanted to find out what their profits were. The first servant reported, 'Master, I invested your money and made ten times the original amount!'

"'Well done!' the king exclaimed. 'You are a good servant. You have been faithful with the little I entrusted to you, so you will be governor of ten cities as your reward.'

"The next servant reported, 'Master, I invested your money and made five times the original amount.'

"'Well done!' the king said. 'You will be governor over five cities.'

"But the third servant brought back only the original amount of money and said, 'Master, I hid your money and kept it safe. I was afraid because you are a hard man to deal with, taking what isn't yours and harvesting crops you didn't plant.'

"'You wicked servant!' the king roared. 'Your own words condemn you. If you knew that I'm a hard man who takes what isn't mine and harvests crops I didn't plant, why didn't you deposit my money in the bank? At least I could have gotten some interest on it.'

"Then, turning to the others standing nearby, the king ordered, 'Take the money from this servant, and give it to the one who has ten pounds.'

" 'But, master,' they said, 'he already has ten pounds!'

" 'Yes,' the king replied, 'and to those who use well what they are given, even more will be given. But from those who do nothing, even what little they have will be taken away. And as for these enemies of mine who didn't want me to be their king—bring them in and execute them right here in front of me.' "

After telling this story, Jesus went on toward Jerusalem, walking ahead of his disciples.

Jerusalem is buzzing about whether Jesus would show His face for the Passover. People have traveled from miles away and have begun their regular Passover preparations. Many, many years before at the first Passover in Egypt, only Jewish homes with the lamb's blood were saved. And now on this Passover, Jesus will shed His blood that can save all people from all nations and ages. He will fulfill his destiny as the Lamb of God, who came to take away the sins of the world.

It was now almost time for the Jewish Passover celebration, and many people from all over the country arrived in Jerusalem several days early so they could go through the purification ceremony before Passover began. They kept looking for Jesus, but as they stood around in the Temple, they said to each other, "What do you think? He won't come for Passover, will he?" Meanwhile, the leading priests and Pharisees had publicly ordered that anyone seeing Jesus must report it immediately so they could arrest him.

Six days before the Passover celebration began, Jesus was in Bethany at the home of Simon, a man who had previously had leprosy. *Bethany was also*[33] the home of Lazarus—the man he had raised from the dead. A dinner was prepared in Jesus' honor. Martha served, and Lazarus was among those who ate with him. Then Mary took a twelve-ounce alabaster jar of expensive perfume made from essence of nard, and broke open the jar and poured the perfume over his head. She anointed Jesus' feet with it, wiping his feet with her hair. The house was filled with the fragrance. But Judas Iscariot, the disciple who would soon betray him, said, "That perfume was worth a year's wages. It should have been sold and the money given to the poor." Not that he cared for the poor—he was a thief, and since he was in charge of the disciples' money, he often stole some for himself.

---

[33] The phrase "Bethany was also" is not part of the NLT text but is a transition to harmonize both Matthew and John's accounts. John emphasizes Bethany as Lazarus's hometown while Matthew tells us that Jesus was anointed in Simon's home.

But Jesus replied, "Leave her alone. Why criticize her for doing such a good thing to me? She did this in preparation for my burial. You will always have the poor among you, and you can help them whenever you want to. But you will not always have me. She has done what she could and has anointed my body for burial ahead of time. I tell you the truth, wherever the Good News is preached throughout the world, this woman's deed will be remembered and discussed."

When all the people heard of Jesus' arrival, they flocked to see him and also to see Lazarus, the man Jesus had raised from the dead. Then the leading priests decided to kill Lazarus, too, for it was because of him that many of the people had deserted them and believed in Jesus.

Jesus knows the suffering that awaits Him in Jerusalem, but He also knows that He must faithfully complete God's mission for Him. So now His journey takes a decisive turn. Jesus heads toward Jerusalem and toward His final destination.

Reflection

Jesus tells another parable of the kingdom of God. What does this one emphasize?

What have you received from the king, Jesus, to invest? What is your investment strategy?

Scripture References

Luke 14:25—19:28; John 11:1—12:11; Matthew 19:1—20:34; 26:6–13; Mark 10:1–52; 14:3–9

His Final Week

202

Travels in His Final Week

After Jesus travels from Bethany to Jerusalem:

1. From the Upper Room (last supper) to the Garden of Gethsemane.

2. From Gethsemane to the house of the Caiaphas (high priest).

3. From the house of Caiaphas to Pilate's judgment hall, then to Herod's palace.

4. From Herod's palace to Pilate.

5. From Pilate's judgment to Golgotha, or Calvary.

6. From Golgotha to the Garden tomb.

7. From Garden tomb to resurrection.

Chapter 10

Jesus' Triumphal Return to Jerusalem

Until now, Jesus walked everywhere He went. Yet, less than two miles from His final destination, He mounts a donkey?! As a fulfillment of prophecy, this triumphal entry demonstrates Jesus' humility and His majesty. As He rides into the city, crowds of people praise Him as their king.

As Jesus and his disciples approached Jerusalem, they came to the towns of Bethphage and Bethany on the Mount of Olives. Jesus sent two of them on ahead. "Go into that village over there," he told them. "As soon as you enter it, you will see a young donkey tied there that no one has ever ridden. Untie it and bring it here. If anyone asks, 'What are you doing?' just say, 'The Lord needs it and will return it soon.' "

The two disciples left and found the colt standing in the street, tied outside the front door. As they were untying it, some bystanders demanded, "What are you doing, untying that colt?" They said what Jesus had told them to say, "The Lord needs it," and they were permitted to take it. Then they brought the colt to Jesus and threw their garments over it, and he sat on it.

This took place to fulfill the prophecy that said,

"Tell the people of Israel, 'Look, your King is coming to you. He is humble, riding on a donkey— riding on a donkey's colt.' "

As he rode along, most of the crowd spread their garments on the road ahead of him, and others cut palm branches from the trees in the fields and spread them on the road.

When they reached the place where the road started down the Mount of Olives, all of his followers began to shout and sing as they walked along, praising God for all the wonderful miracles they had seen.

Jesus was in the center of the procession, and the people all around him were shouting,

"Praise God for the Son of David! Blessings on the one who comes in the name of the LORD! Praise God in highest heaven!"

His disciples didn't understand at the time that this was a fulfillment of prophecy. But after Jesus entered into his glory, they remembered what had happened and realized that these things had been written about him.

Many in the crowd had seen Jesus call Lazarus from the tomb, raising him from the dead, and they were telling others about it. That was the reason so many went out to meet him—because they had heard about this miraculous sign.

But some of the Pharisees among the crowd said, "Teacher, rebuke your followers for saying things like that!"

He replied, "If they kept quiet, the stones along the road would burst into cheers!"

Then the Pharisees said to each other, "There's nothing we can do. Look, everyone has gone after him!"

But as they came closer to Jerusalem and Jesus saw the city ahead, he began to weep. "How I wish today that you of all people would understand the way to peace. But now it is too late, and peace is hidden from your eyes. Before long your enemies will build ramparts against your walls and encircle you and close in on you from every side. They will crush you into the ground, and your children with you. Your enemies will not leave a single stone in place, because you did not accept your opportunity for salvation."

The entire city of Jerusalem was in an uproar as he entered. "Who is this?" they asked.

And the crowds replied, "It's Jesus, the prophet from Nazareth in Galilee."

The blind and the lame came to him in the Temple, and he healed them. The leading priests and the teachers of religious law saw these wonderful miracles and heard even the children in the Temple shouting, "Praise God for the Son of David."

But the leaders were indignant. They asked Jesus, "Do you hear what these children are saying?"

"Yes," Jesus replied. "Haven't you ever read the Scriptures? For they say, ' You have taught children and infants to give you praise.' "

After looking around carefully at everything, he left because it was late in the afternoon. Then he returned to Bethany with the twelve disciples.

The next morning as they were leaving Bethany, Jesus was hungry. He noticed a fig tree in full leaf a little way off, so he went over to see if he could find any figs. But there were only leaves because it was too early in the season for fruit. Then Jesus said to the tree, "May no one ever eat your fruit again!" And

the disciples heard him say it. And immediately the
fig tree withered up.

*In all the excitement of Sunday, Jesus apparently
forgets to eat dinner. So spotting a fig tree full of
leaves on Monday morning means it's breakfast
time. But Jesus discovers that His breakfast tree
that appears to be full of fruit is really just a
pretty tree with lots of leaves and no fruit. In His
frustration, Jesus seizes this teachable moment.
Because the tree fails to fulfill its God-given
purpose of producing fruit, it is judged swiftly and
harshly by Jesus. In the same way, Jesus and His
disciples will soon enter God's Temple that is
failing to serve its purpose as a house of prayer.
Instead it has become a house of greed. Being in
the Temple will not protect those responsible from
suffering the same fate as the fig tree.*

When they arrived back in Jerusalem, Jesus
entered the Temple and began to drive out all the
people buying and selling animals for sacrifices. He
knocked over the tables of the money changers and
the chairs of those selling doves, and he stopped
everyone from using the Temple as a marketplace.
He said to them, "The Scriptures declare, 'My
Temple will be called a house of prayer for all
nations,' but you have turned it into a den of
thieves."

When the leading priests and teachers of
religious law heard what Jesus had done, they began
planning how to kill him. But they were afraid of
him because all the people hung on every word he
said and were so amazed at his teaching.

Some Greeks who had come to Jerusalem for
the Passover celebration paid a visit to Philip, who

was from Bethsaida in Galilee. They said, "Sir, we want to meet Jesus." Philip told Andrew about it, and they went together to ask Jesus.

Jesus replied, "Now the time has come for the Son of Man to enter into his glory. I tell you the truth, unless a kernel of wheat is planted in the soil and dies, it remains alone. But its death will produce many new kernels—a plentiful harvest of new lives. Those who love their life in this world will lose it. Those who care nothing for their life in this world will keep it for eternity. Anyone who wants to be my disciple must follow me, because my servants must be where I am. And the Father will honor anyone who serves me.

"Now my soul is deeply troubled. Should I pray, 'Father, save me from this hour'? But this is the very reason I came! Father, bring glory to your name."

Then a voice spoke from heaven, saying, "I have already brought glory to my name, and I will do so again." When the crowd heard the voice, some thought it was thunder, while others declared an angel had spoken to him.

Then Jesus told them, "The voice was for your benefit, not mine. The time for judging this world has come, when Satan, the ruler of this world, will be cast out. And when I am lifted up from the earth, I will draw everyone to myself." He said this to indicate how he was going to die.

The crowd responded, "We understood from Scripture that the Messiah would live forever. How can you say the Son of Man will die? Just who is this Son of Man, anyway?"

Jesus replied, "My light will shine for you just a little longer. Walk in the light while you can, so the darkness will not overtake you. Those who walk in the darkness cannot see where they are going. Put your trust in the light while there is still time; then you will become children of the light."

After saying these things, Jesus went away and was hidden from them.

But despite all the miraculous signs Jesus had done, most of the people still did not believe in him. This is exactly what Isaiah the prophet had predicted: "LORD, who has believed our message? To whom has the LORD revealed his powerful arm?" But the people couldn't believe, for as Isaiah also said,

> "The Lord has blinded their eyes and hardened their hearts—so that their eyes cannot see, and their hearts cannot understand, and they cannot turn to me and have me heal them."

Isaiah was referring to Jesus when he said this, because he saw the future and spoke of the Messiah's glory. Many people did believe in him, however, including some of the Jewish leaders. But they wouldn't admit it for fear that the Pharisees would expel them from the synagogue. For they loved human praise more than the praise of God.

Jesus shouted to the crowds, "If you trust me, you are trusting not only me, but also God who sent me. For when you see me, you are seeing the one who sent me. I have come as a light to shine in this dark world, so that all who put their trust in me will no longer remain in the dark. I will not judge those who hear me but don't obey me, for I have come to save the world and not to judge it. But all who reject me and my message will be judged on the day of judgment by the truth I have spoken. I don't speak on my own authority. The Father who sent me has commanded me what to say and how to say it. And I know his commands lead to eternal life; so I say whatever the Father tells me to say."

That evening Jesus and the disciples left the city.

The next morning as they passed by the fig tree he had cursed, the disciples noticed it had withered from the roots up. Peter remembered what Jesus had said to the tree on the previous day and exclaimed, "Look, Rabbi! The fig tree you cursed has withered and died!"

Then Jesus said to the disciples, "Have faith in God.

Then Jesus told them, "I tell you the truth, if you have faith and don't doubt, you can do things like this and much more. You can even say to this mountain, 'May you be lifted up and thrown into the sea,' and it will happen.

"I tell you, you can pray for anything, and if you believe that you've received it, it will be yours. But when you are praying, first forgive anyone you are holding a grudge against, so that your Father in heaven will forgive your sins, too."

Every day Jesus went to the Temple to teach, and each evening he returned to spend the night on the Mount of Olives. The crowds gathered at the Temple early each morning to hear him.

Reflection

As Jesus rode into Jerusalem what were people's responses to Him? What was His response to what was happening?

A healthy fig tree produces fruit before leaves. Are there areas in your life that look good, but may not have real fruit of the spirit?

*Tuesday begins by passing the same fig tree that
was cursed on Monday. This day would once
again be filled with confrontation. After refusing
to answer people who simply refuse to believe,
Jesus proceeds to tell three different parables about
people who reject the Messiah, and the
punishment they will receive.*

Again they entered Jerusalem. As Jesus was
walking through the Temple area teaching the
people and preaching the Good News, the leading
priests, the teachers of religious law, and he elders
came up to him. They demanded, "By what
authority are you doing all these things? Who gave
you the right to do them?"

"I'll tell you by what authority I do these things
if you answer one question," Jesus replied. "Did
John's authority to baptize come from heaven, or
was it merely human? Answer me!"

They talked it over among themselves. "If we
say it was from heaven, he will ask us why we didn't
believe John. But if we say it was merely human,
we'll be mobbed and the people will stone us
because the people believe John was a prophet." So
they finally replied, "We don't know."

And Jesus responded, "Then I won't tell you by
what authority I do these things.

"But what do you think about this? A man with
two sons told the older boy, 'Son, go out and work
in the vineyard today.' The son answered, ' No, I
won't go,' but later he changed his mind and went
anyway. Then the father told the other son, ' You
go,' and he said, ' Yes, sir, I will.' But he didn't go.

"Which of the two obeyed his father?"

They replied, "The first."

Then Jesus explained his meaning: "I tell you the truth, corrupt tax collectors and prostitutes will get into the Kingdom of God before you do. For John the Baptist came and showed you the right way to live, but you didn't believe him, while tax collectors and prostitutes did. And even when you saw this hap-pening, you refused to believe him and repent of your sins.

"Now listen to another story. A certain landowner planted a vineyard, built a wall around it, dug a pit for pressing out the grape juice, and built a lookout tower. Then he leased the vineyard to tenant farmers and moved to another country. At the time of the grape harvest, he sent his servants to collect his share of the crop. But the farmers grabbed his servants, beat one, killed one, and stoned another. So the landowner sent a larger group of his servants to collect for him, but the results were the same.

"Finally, the owner sent his son, thinking, 'Surely they will respect my son.'

"But when the tenant farmers saw his son coming, they said to one another, 'Here comes the heir to this estate. Come on, let's kill him and get the estate for ourselves!' So they grabbed him, dragged him out of the vineyard, and murdered him.

"How terrible that such a thing should ever happen," his listeners protested.

"When the owner of the vineyard returns," Jesus asked, "what do you think he will do to those farmers?"

The religious leaders replied, "He will put the wicked men to a horrible death and lease the vineyard to others who will give him his share of the crop after each harvest."

Then Jesus asked them, "Didn't you ever read this in the Scriptures?

'The stone that the builders rejected has now become the cornerstone. This is the LORD's doing, and it is wonderful to see.'

I tell you, the Kingdom of God will be taken away from you and given to a nation that will produce the proper fruit. Anyone who stumbles over that stone will be broken to pieces, and it will crush anyone it falls on."

When the leading priests and Pharisees heard this parable, they realized he was telling the story against them—they were the wicked farmers. They wanted to arrest him, but they were afraid of the crowds, who considered Jesus to be a prophet, so they left him and went away.

Jesus also told them other parables. He said, "The Kingdom of Heaven can be illustrated by the story of a king who prepared a great wedding feast for his son. When the banquet was ready, he sent his servants to notify those who were invited. But they all refused to come!

"So he sent other servants to tell them, ' The feast has been prepared. The bulls and fattened cattle have been killed, and everything is ready. Come to the banquet!' But the guests he had invited ignored them and went their own way, one to his farm, another to his business. Others seized his messengers and insulted them and killed them.

"The king was furious, and he sent out his army to destroy the murderers and burn their town. And he said to his servants, ' The wedding feast is ready, and the guests I invited aren't worthy of the honor. Now go out to the street corners and invite everyone you see.' So the servants brought in everyone they could find, good and bad alike, and the banquet hall was filled with guests.

"But when the king came in to meet the guests, he noticed a man who wasn't wearing the proper clothes for a wedding. 'Friend,' he asked, 'how is it that you are here without wedding clothes?' But the man had no reply. Then the king said to his aides, 'Bind his hands and feet and throw him into the outer darkness, where there will be weeping and gnashing of teeth.' "For many are called, but few are chosen."

Jesus' indictment against those who reject Him is not lost on His enemies. The Herodians, Sadducees, and Pharisees now unite in their interrogation of Jesus. However, this new attempt to discredit Him will only further demonstrate Jesus' wisdom and authority.

Then the Pharisees met together to plot how to trap Jesus into saying something that could be reported to the Roman governor so he could arrest Jesus. They sent some of their disciples, spies pretending to be honest men, along with the supporters of Herod, to meet with him. "Teacher," they said, "we know how honest you are. You teach the way of God truthfully. You are impartial and don't play favorites. Now tell us what you think about this: Is it right to pay taxes to Caesar or not?"

But Jesus knew their evil motives. "You hypocrites!" he said. "Why are you trying to trap me? Here, show me the coin used for the tax." When they handed him a Roman coin, he asked, "Whose picture and title are stamped on it?"

"Caesar's," they replied.

Reflection

👁 To whom does Jesus speak most in these passages? What is he challenging?

✋ The crowds gather to hear Jesus; the religious leaders question Jesus. Which camp do you lean towards in this season of your life?

"Well, then," he said, "give to Caesar what belongs to Caesar, and give to God what belongs to God."

So they failed to trap him by what he said in front of the people. Instead, they were amazed by his answer, and they became silent and went away.

Then that same day Jesus was approached by some Sadducees—religious leaders who say there is no resurrection from the dead. They posed this question: "Teacher, Moses gave us a law that if a man dies, leaving a wife without children, his brother should marry the widow and have a child who will carry on the brother's name. Well, suppose there were seven brothers. The oldest one married and then died without children. So the second brother married the widow, but he also died without children. Then the third brother married her. This continued with all seven of them, and still there were no children. Last of all, the woman also died. So tell us, whose wife will she be in the resurrection? For all seven were married to her."

Jesus replied, "Your mistake is that you don't know the Scriptures, and you don't know the power of God. Marriage is for people here on earth. But in the age to come, those worthy of being raised from the dead will neither marry nor be given in marriage. And they will never die again. In this respect they will be like angels. They are children of God and children of the resurrection.

"But now, as to whether the dead will be raised—haven't you ever read about this in the writings of Moses, in the story of the burning bush?

Long after Abraham, Isaac, and Jacob had died, he referred to the Lord as 'the God of Abraham, the God of Isaac, and the God of Jacob.' So he is the God of the living, not the dead, for they are all alive to him."

When the crowds heard him, they were astounded at his teaching.

"Well said, Teacher!" remarked some of the teachers of religious law who were standing there. And then no one dared to ask him any more questions.

But when the Pharisees heard that he had silenced the Sadducees with his reply, they met together to question him again.

One of the teachers, an expert in religious law, was standing there listening to the debate. He realized that Jesus had answered well, so he asked, "Of all the commandments, which is the most important?"

Jesus replied, "The most important commandment is this: 'Listen, O Israel! The LORD our God is the one and only LORD. And you must love the LORD your God with all your heart, all your soul, all your mind, and all your strength.' This is the first and greatest commandment. The second is equally important: 'Love your neighbor as yourself.' No other commandment is greater than these. The entire law and all the demands of the prophets are based on these two commandments."

Then, surrounded by the Pharisees, Jesus asked them a question: "What do you think about the Messiah? Whose son is he?"

They replied, "He is the son of David."

Jesus responded, "Then why does David, speaking under the inspiration of the Spirit, call the Messiah 'my Lord'? For David said,

'The LORD said to my Lord, Sit in the place of honor at my right hand until I humble your enemies beneath your feet.'

Since David called the Messiah 'my Lord,' how can the Messiah be his son?"

No one could answer him. The large crowd listened to him with great delight. And after that, no one dared to ask him any more questions.

Tuesday has been a long day, but Jesus isn't finished. Now that Jesus has everyone's attention, it's time for Him to go on the offensive. This isn't a personal vendetta, and Jesus doesn't have a chip on His shoulder. Jesus is seriously concerned for the victims of these false teachers. When the minds of innocent people are being poisoned, the only choice Jesus has is to attack the real problem in the strongest possible way.

Then Jesus said to the crowds and to his disciples, "The teachers of religious law and the Pharisees are the official interpreters of the law of Moses. So practice and obey whatever they tell you, but don't follow their example. For they don't practice what they teach. They crush people with impossible religious demands and never lift a finger to ease the burden.

"Everything they do is for show. On their arms they wear extra wide prayer boxes with Scripture verses inside, and they wear robes with extra long tassels. And they love to sit at the head table at banquets and in the seats of honor in the synagogues. They love to receive respectful greetings as they walk in the marketplaces, and to be called 'Rabbi.'

"Don't let anyone call you 'Rabbi,' for you have only one teacher, and all of you are equal as brothers and sisters. And don't address anyone here on earth as 'Father,' for only God in heaven is your spiritual Father. And don't let anyone call you ' Teacher,' for you have only one teacher, the Messiah. The greatest among you must be a servant. But those who exalt themselves will be humbled, and those who humble themselves will be exalted.

"What sorrow awaits you teachers of religious law and you Pharisees. Hypocrites! For you shut the door of the Kingdom of Heaven in people's faces. You won't go in yourselves, and you don't let others enter either. Yet you shamelessly cheat widows out of their property and then pretend to be pious by making long prayers in public. Because of this, you will be more severely punished.

"What sorrow awaits you teachers of religious law and you Pharisees. Hypocrites! For you cross land and sea to make one convert, and then you turn that person into twice the child of hell you yourselves are!

"Blind guides! What sorrow awaits you! For you say that it means nothing to swear 'by God's Temple,' but that it is binding to swear 'by the gold in the Temple.' Blind fools! Which is more important—the gold or the Temple that makes the gold sacred? And you say that to swear 'by the altar' is not binding, but to swear 'by the gifts on the altar' is binding. How blind! For which is more important—the gift on the altar or the altar that makes the gift sacred? When you swear 'by the altar,'

you are swearing by it and by everything on it. And
when you swear 'by the Temple,' you are swearing
by it and by God, who lives in it. And when you
swear 'by heaven,' you are swearing by the throne of
God and by God, who sits on the throne.

"What sorrow awaits you teachers of religious
law and you Pharisees. Hypocrites! For you are
careful to tithe even the tiniest income from your
herb gardens, but you ignore the more important
aspects of the law—justice, mercy, and faith. You
should tithe, yes, but do not neglect the more
important things. Blind guides! You strain your
water so you won't accidentally swallow a gnat, but
you swallow a camel!

"What sorrow awaits you teachers of religious
law and you Pharisees. Hypocrites! For you are so
careful to clean the outside of the cup and the dish,
but inside you are filthy—full of greed and self-
indulgence! You blind Pharisee! First wash the inside
of the cup and the dish, and then the outside will
become clean, too.

"What sorrow awaits you teachers of religious
law and you Pharisees. Hypocrites! For you are like
whitewashed tombs—beautiful on the outside but
filled on the inside with dead people's bones and all
sorts of impurity. Outwardly you look like righteous
people, but inwardly your hearts are filled with
hypocrisy and lawlessness.

"What sorrow awaits you teachers of religious
law and you Pharisees. Hypocrites! For you build
tombs for the prophets your ancestors killed, and
you decorate the monuments of the godly people
your ancestors destroyed. Then you say, 'If we had
lived in the days of our ancestors, we would never
have joined them in killing the prophets.'

"But in saying that, you testify against yourselves that you are indeed the descendants of those who murdered the prophets. Go ahead and finish what your ancestors started. Snakes! Sons of vipers! How will you escape the judgment of hell?

"Therefore, I am sending you prophets and wise men and teachers of religious law. But you will kill some by crucifixion, and you will flog others with whips in your synagogues, chasing them from city to city. As a result, you will be held responsible for the murder of all godly people of all time—from the murder of righteous Abel to the murder of Zechariah son of Barachiah, whom you killed in the Temple between the sanctuary and the altar. I tell you the truth, this judgment will fall on this very generation.

"O Jerusalem, Jerusalem, the city that kills the prophets and stones God's messengers! How often I have wanted to gather your children together as a hen protects her chicks beneath her wings, but you wouldn't let me. And now, look, your house is abandoned and desolate. For I tell you this, you will never see me again until you say, 'Blessings on the one who comes in the name of the LORD!' "

Jesus sat down near the collection box in the Temple and watched as the crowds dropped in their money. Many rich people put in large amounts. Then a poor widow came and dropped in two small coins.

Jesus called his disciples to him and said, "I tell you the truth, this poor widow has given more than all the others who are making contributions. For they gave a tiny part of their surplus, but she, poor as she is, has given everything she had to live on."

Jesus doesn't enjoy lambasting the Pharisees. He weeps over their fate and that of those who follow their ways. After detailing the problem with empty religion, Jesus concludes with a positive example. In His typical simple yet shocking manner, Jesus points to the poor widow's small offering as the example of great faith. Now Jesus will shift his teaching onto the future. Like most prophecies, His predictions have both immediate and distant implications. The immediate is the destruction of Jerusalem at the hands of Rome in A.D. 70. The distant is the final judgment of mankind at the end of time.

Reflection

How does Jesus respond when asked about the law and commandments?

Jesus said a widow's giving was significant. What does giving look like for you?

As Jesus was leaving the Temple grounds, his disciples pointed out to him the various Temple buildings, "Teacher, look at these magnificent buildings! Look at the impressive stones in the walls."

But he responded, "Do you see all these buildings? I tell you the truth, they will be completely demolished. Not one stone will be left on top of another!"

Later, Jesus sat on the Mount of Olives. His disciples came to him privately and said, "Tell us, when will all this happen? What sign will signal your return and the end of the world?"

Jesus told them, "Don't let anyone mislead you, for many will come in my name, claiming, 'I am the Messiah,' and 'The time has come!' They will deceive many. But don't believe them. And you will hear of wars and threats of wars, but don't panic. Yes, these things must take place first, but the end won't follow immediately. Nation will go to war against nation, and kingdom against kingdom. There will be famines and earthquakes in many parts of the world, and there will be terrifying things and great miraculous signs from heaven. But all this is only the first of the birth pains, with more to come.

"When these things begin to happen, watch out! Before all this occurs, there will be a time of great persecution. You will be dragged into local councils and beaten in the synagogues and prisons, and you will stand trial before kings and governors because you are my followers. But this will be your opportunity to tell them about me. So don't worry in advance about how to answer the charges against you, for I will give you the right words and such wisdom that none of your opponents will be able to reply or refute you, for it is not you who will be speaking, but the Holy Spirit! Even those closest to you—your parents, brothers, relatives, and friends— will betray you. They will even kill some of you. And everyone will hate you because you are my followers. But not a hair of your head will perish!

"And many will turn away from me and betray and hate each other. And many false prophets will appear and will deceive many people. Sin will be rampant everywhere, and the love of many will grow cold. But the one who endures to the end will be saved. And the Good News about the Kingdom will be preached throughout the whole world, so that all nations will hear it; and then the end will come.

"The day is coming when you will see what Daniel the prophet spoke about—the sacrilegious object that causes desecration standing in the Holy

Place.[34] (Reader, pay attention!) And when you see
Jerusalem surrounded by armies, then you will know
that the time of its destruction has arrived. Then
those in Judea must flee to the hills. A person out on
the deck of a roof must not go down into the house
to pack. A person out in the field must not return
even to get a coat. Those in Jerusalem must get out,
and those out in the country should not return to the
city. For those will be days of God's vengeance, and
the prophetic words of the Scriptures will be
fulfilled. For there will be disaster in the land and
great anger against this people. They will be killed by
the sword or sent away as captives to all the nations
of the world. And Jerusalem will be trampled down
by the Gentiles until the period of the Gentiles
comes to an end. "How terrible it will be for
pregnant women and for nursing mothers in those
days. And pray that your flight will not be in winter
or on the Sabbath. For there will be greater anguish
than at any time since the world began. And it will
never be so great again. In fact, unless that time of
calamity is shortened, not a single person will
survive. But it will be shortened for the sake of
God's chosen ones.

---

[34] This term is used in the Old Testament by Daniel in
chapters 9, 11, and 13. It was a phrase that represented an
action or entity which causes both sacrilege and destruction.
Daniel predicted that this destruction would happen in the
Temple. Daniel's prophecy was fulfilled in 163 B.C. by
Antiochus Epiphanes, who entered the Temple with his
Syrian armies and murdered worshipers and allowed his
troops to fornicate in the Temple. It was fulfilled again in 63
B.C. when the Roman general Pompey ransacked the city and
actually entered the Holy of Holies. But Jesus quotes the term
for His teaching referring to a future fulfillment. The
destruction of Jerusalem in A.D. 70 would certainly fit this
description (see *Wars* by Josephus).

"Then if anyone tells you, 'Look, here is the Messiah,' or 'There he is,' don't believe it. For false messiahs and false prophets will rise up and perform great signs and wonders so as to deceive, if possible, even God's chosen ones. Watch out! See, I have warned you about this ahead of time.

"So if someone tells you, 'Look, the Messiah is out in the desert,' don't bother to go and look. Or, 'Look, he is hiding here,' don't believe it! For as the lightning flashes in the east and shines to the west, so it will be when the Son of Man comes. Just as the gathering of vultures[35] shows there is a carcass nearby, so these signs indicate that the end is near.

"Immediately after the anguish of those days,

the sun will be darkened, the moon will give no light, the stars will fall from the sky, and the powers in the heavens will be shaken.

"And there will be strange signs in the sun, moon, and stars. And here on earth the nations will be in turmoil, perplexed by the roaring seas and strange tides. People will be terrified at what they see coming upon the earth, for the powers in the heavens will be shaken.

"And then at last, the sign that the Son of Man is coming will appear in the heavens, and there will be deep mourning among all the peoples of the

---

[35] **vultures:** Jesus has now shifted from talking about the destruction of Jerusalem in A.D. 70 to talking about judgment at the end of time. By using the term "the gathering of vultures" Jesus is referring to the obvious nature of His Second Coming. Just like circling vultures make it obvious that there is something dead below, God's judgment against sin will be something no one will miss.

earth. And they will see the Son of Man coming on the clouds of heaven with power and great glory. And he will send out his angels with the mighty blast of a trumpet, and they will gather his chosen ones from all over the world—from the farthest ends of the earth and heaven.

"Now learn a lesson from the fig tree. When its branches bud and its leaves begin to sprout, you know that summer is near. In the same way, when you see all these things, stand and look up, for your salvation is near! You can know his return is very near, right at the door. I tell you the truth, this generation will not pass from the scene until all these things take place. Heaven and earth will disappear, but my words will never disappear.

"However, no one knows the day or hour when these things will happen, not even the angels in heaven or the Son himself. Only the Father knows.

"When the Son of Man returns, it will be like it was in Noah's day. In those days before the flood, the people were enjoying banquets and parties and weddings right up to the time Noah entered his boat. People didn't realize what was going to happen until the flood came and swept them all away. That is the way it will be when the Son of Man comes.

"Two men will be working together in the field; one will be taken, the other left. Two women will be grinding flour at the mill; one will be taken, the other left.

"Watch out! Don't let your hearts be dulled by carousing and drunkenness, and by the worries of this life. Don't let that day catch you unaware, like a trap. For that day will come upon everyone living on the earth. Keep alert at all times. And pray that you might be strong enough to escape these coming horrors and stand before the Son of Man.

"The coming of the Son of Man can be illustrated by the story of a man going on a long trip. When he left home, he gave each of his slaves instructions about the work they were to do, and he told the gatekeeper to watch for his return.

"So you, too, must keep watch! For you don't know what day your Lord is coming. Understand this: If a homeowner knew exactly when a burglar was coming, he would keep watch and not permit his house to be broken into. You also must be ready all the time, for the Son of Man will come when least expected.

"A faithful, sensible servant is one to whom the master can give the responsibility of managing his other household servants and feeding them. If the master returns and finds that the servant has done a good job, there will be a reward. I tell you the truth, the master will put that servant in charge of all he owns. But what if the servant is evil and thinks, 'My master won't be back for a while,' and he begins beating the other servants, partying, and getting drunk? The master will return unannounced and unexpected, and he will cut the servant to pieces and assign him a place with the hypocrites. In that place there will be weeping and gnashing of teeth.

Reflection

What assurances and cautions does Jesus give regarding the end of times?

How can you 'keep alert and be ready' for Jesus' return while you faithfully live each day?

"The Kingdom of Heaven will be like ten bridesmaids who took their lamps and went to meet the bridegroom. Five of them were foolish, and five were wise. The five who were foolish didn't take enough olive oil for their lamps, but the other five were wise enough to take along extra oil. When the bridegroom was delayed, they all became drowsy and fell asleep.

"At midnight they were roused by the shout, 'Look, the bridegroom is coming! Come out and meet him!'

"All the bridesmaids got up and prepared their lamps. Then the five foolish ones asked the others, 'Please give us some of your oil because our lamps are going out.'

"But the others replied, 'We don't have enough for all of us. Go to a shop and buy some for yourselves.'

"But while they were gone to buy oil, the bridegroom came. Then those who were ready went in with him to the marriage feast, and the door was locked. Later, when the other five bridesmaids returned, they stood outside, calling, 'Lord! Lord! Open the door for us!'

"But he called back, 'Believe me, I don't know you!'

"So you, too, must keep watch! For you do not know the day or hour of my return.

"Again, the Kingdom of Heaven can be illustrated by the story of a man going on a long trip. He called together his servants and entrusted his money to them while he was gone. He gave five bags of silver to one, two bags of silver to another, and one bag of silver to the last—dividing it in proportion to their abilities. He then left on his trip.

"The servant who received the five bags of silver began to invest the money and earned five more. The servant with two bags of silver also went to work and earned two more. But the servant who received the one bag of silver dug a hole in the ground and hid the master's money.

"After a long time their master returned from his trip and called them to give an account of how they had used his money. The servant to whom he had entrusted the five bags of silver came forward with five more and said, 'Master, you gave me five bags of silver to invest, and I have earned five more.'

"The master was full of praise. 'Well done, my good and faithful servant. You have been faithful in handling this small amount, so now I will give you many more responsibilities. Let's celebrate together!'

"The servant who had received the two bags of silver came forward and said, 'Master, you gave me two bags of silver to invest, and I have earned two more.'

"The master said, 'Well done, my good and faithful servant. You have been faithful in handling this small amount, so now I will give you many more responsibilities. Let's celebrate together!'

"Then the servant with the one bag of silver came and said, 'Master, I knew you were a harsh man, harvesting crops you didn't plant and gathering crops you didn't cultivate. I was afraid I would lose your money, so I hid it in the earth. Look, here is your money back.'

"But the master replied, 'You wicked and lazy servant! If you knew I harvested crops I didn't plant and gathered crops I didn't cultivate, why didn't you deposit my money in the bank? At least I could have gotten some interest on it.'

"Then he ordered, 'Take the money from this servant, and give it to the one with the ten bags of silver. To those who use well what they are given, even more will be given, and they will have an abundance. But from those who do nothing, even what little they have will be taken away. Now throw this useless servant into outer darkness, where there will be weeping and gnashing of teeth.'

"But when the Son of Man comes in his glory, and all the angels with him, then he will sit upon his glorious throne. All the nations will be gathered in his presence, and he will separate the people as a shepherd separates the sheep from the goats. He will place the sheep at his right hand and the goats at his left.

"Then the King will say to those on his right, 'Come, you who are blessed by my Father, inherit the Kingdom prepared for you from the creation of the world. For I was hungry, and you fed me. I was thirsty, and you gave me a drink. I was a stranger, and you invited me into your home. I was naked, and you gave me clothing. I was sick, and you cared for me. I was in prison, and you visited me.'

"Then these righteous ones will reply, 'Lord, when did we ever see you hungry and feed you? Or thirsty and give you something to drink? Or a stranger and show you hospitality? Or naked and give you clothing? When did we ever see you sick or in prison and visit you?'

"And the King will say, 'I tell you the truth, when you did it to one of the least of these my brothers and sisters, you were doing it to me!'

"Then the King will turn to those on the left and say, 'Away with you, you cursed ones, into the eternal fire prepared for the devil and his demons. For I was hungry, and you didn't feed me. I was thirsty, and you didn't give me a drink. I was a stranger, and you didn't invite me into your home. I was naked, and you didn't give me clothing. I was sick and in prison, and you didn't visit me.'

"Then they will reply, 'Lord, when did we ever see you hungry or thirsty or a stranger or naked or sick or in prison, and not help you?'

"And he will answer, 'I tell you the truth, when you refused to help the least of these my brothers and sisters, you were refusing to help me.'

"And they will go away into eternal punishment, but the righteous will go into eternal life."

When Jesus had finished saying all these things, he said to his disciples, "As you know, Passover begins in two days, and the Son of Man will be handed over to be crucified."

At that same time the leading priests and elders were meeting at the residence of Caiaphas, the high priest, plotting how to capture Jesus secretly and kill him. "But not during the Passover celebration," they agreed, "or the people may riot." Then Satan entered into Judas Iscariot, who was one of the twelve disciples, and he went to the leading priests and captains of the Temple guard to discuss the best way to betray Jesus to them, and asked, "How much will you pay me to betray Jesus to you?" They were delighted when they heard why he had come, and they gave him thirty pieces of silver. So he agreed and began looking for an opportunity to betray Jesus so they could arrest him when the crowds weren't around.

Reflection

What are the two parables Jesus teaches here?

How do you recognize and wisely invest what God has given you? Where does 'fear' creep into your life?

Scripture References

Matthew 21:1—26:16; Mark 11:1—14:11;
Luke 19:29—22:6; 21:37–38; John 12:12–
50

Chapter 11

The Upper Room and Passover

It is now Thursday. The Passover and Festival of Unleavened Bread (two feasts virtually celebrated as one in Jesus' time) was a seven-day memorial to the exodus. Faithful Jewish worshipers gather in Jerusalem from all over the Roman Empire. Some estimate as many as a million people packed into the city, requiring approximately 100,000 sacrificial lambs. The disciples may not realize it yet, but this night will be powerful. Its symbolism is rich, its raw emotion is visceral, and its teaching is life-changing! Come . . . into the upper room!

On the first day of the Festival of Unleavened Bread,[36] when the Passover lamb is sacrificed, Jesus' disciples asked him, "Where do you want us to go to prepare the Passover[37] meal for you?"

So Jesus sent two of them, Peter and John, into Jerusalem with these instructions: "As you go into the city, a man carrying a pitcher of water will meet

---

[36] **Festival of Unleavened Bread**: The Festival of Unleavened Bread immediately followed the Passover and lasted seven days, from the 15th to the 21st of Nisan (or Abib). On each of those days, after the morning sacrifice, a sacrifice in connection with the feast was presented; unleavened bread alone was eaten (Exodus 12:15–20; 13:6–7; Deuteronomy 16:3–8).

[37] **Passover**: An important holy day for the Jews in the spring of each year. They ate a special meal on this day to remind them that God had freed them from being slaves in Egypt. The first Passover was recorded in Exodus 12:1–30. God also commanded that it be celebrated in Numbers 9:1–14. It was also celebrated by Jesus in Matthew 26:2, 17–19.

you. Follow him. At the house he enters, say to the owner, 'The Teacher says: My time has come. Where is the guest room where I can eat the Passover meal with my disciples?' He will take you upstairs to a large room that is already set up. That is where you should prepare our meal." So the two disciples went into the city and found everything just as Jesus had said, and they prepared the Passover meal there.

When the time came, Jesus and the apostles sat down together at the table. Jesus said, "I have been very eager to eat this Passover meal with you before my suffering begins. For I tell you now that I won't eat this meal again until its meaning is fulfilled in the Kingdom of God."

> *They took their places around a U-shaped set of low tables about ten inches off the floor. They "reclined" on their left elbows on cushions around the perimeter of the table. For Jesus this is much more than a festive meal. It is much more than a normal Passover celebration. Jesus knows this meal commemorates His imminent destiny to die on the cross. It is the last time He will participate in the Passover as a man, but there will be another banquet, a wedding feast, that will take place in the future!*

Passover

Offering of the Paschal Lamb. *The lamb was to be free from all blemish and neither less than eight days nor more than exactly one year old. Each paschal lamb was to serve a "company" of not less than ten nor more than twenty, the representatives of each company going to the Temple. The daily evening sacrifice (Exodus 29:38–39), usually killed at the eighth and a half hour (i.e., 2:30 p.m.), and offered up at the ninth and a half hour (i.e., 3:30 p.m.), was on this day killed at 1:30 and offered at 2:30 p.m., an hour earlier. And if the 14th of Nisan happened on a Friday, it was killed at 12:30 and offered at 1:30 p.m., two hours earlier than usual, so as to avoid any needless breach of the Sabbath.*

The Passover Supper. *As the guests gathered around the paschal table they were arrayed in their best festive garments, joyous and at rest, as became the children of a king. To express this idea the rabbis insisted that at least a part of the feast should be partaken in a recumbent position. The left elbow was placed on the table, the head resting on the hand, with sufficient room between each guest for the free movement of the right hand. This explains in what sense John was reclining on Jesus' breast, and afterward leaning back thus on Jesus' breast when he leaned back to speak to Him (John 13:23, 25; Luke 22:14). The father, or other person presiding, took the place of honor at the table, probably somewhat raised above the rest.*

The paschal supper commenced by the head of the "company" pronouncing a benediction over the first cup of wine, which had been filled for each person. It was then drunk, and a basin of water and a towel were handed around or the guests got up to wash their hands (John 13:4–5, 12), after which the appropriate blessing was pronounced.

These preliminaries ended, a table was brought in, upon which was the paschal meal. The president of the feast first took some of the herbs, dipped them in the sauce (Heb. charoseth), ate some, and gave to the others (Matthew 26:23; John 13:26). Immediately after this all the dishes were removed from the table (to excite curiosity), and the second cup of wine was filled. Then the son asked his father as follows: "Wherefore is this night distinguished from all other nights? For on all other nights we eat leavened or unleavened bread, but on this night only unleavened bread? On all other nights we eat any kind of herbs, but on this night only bitter herbs? On all other nights we eat meat roasted, stewed, or boiled but on this night only roasted? On all other nights we dip [the herbs] only once, but on this night twice?" In reply the head of the house related the whole national history, commencing with Terah, Abraham's father, Israel's deliverance from Egypt, and the giving of the law.

The paschal dishes were now placed back upon the table. The president took up in succession the dish with the Passover lamb, that with the bitter herbs, and that with the unleavened bread, briefly explaining the importance of each; the first part of the Hallel was sung (Psalm 113–114), with this brief thanksgiving at the close: "Blessed art thou, Jehovah our God, King of the universe, who hast redeemed us and redeemed our fathers from Egypt." The second cup of wine was then drunk, and hands were washed a second time, with the same prayer as before, and one of the two unleavened cakes broken and "thanks given."

Pieces of the broken cake, with "bitter herbs" between them and "dipped" in the charoseth, were next handed to each of the company. This, in all probability, was the "dipped morsel" which, in answer to John's inquiry about the betrayer, the Lord "gave" to Judas (John 13:25–30; cf. Mark 14:22; Luke 22:21).

The paschal supper itself consisted of the unleavened bread, with bitter herbs, of the so-called Chagigah (i.e., a voluntary peace offering made by private individuals), and the paschal lamb itself. After that nothing more was to be eaten, so that the flesh of the paschal sacrifice might be the last meat partaken of. But since the cessation of the paschal sacrifice, the Jews conclude the supper with a piece of unleavened cake called the Aphikomen, or after dish. Hands were again washed, the third cup was filled, and grace after meat said. The service concluded with the fourth cups over which the second portion of the Hallel was sung (Psalm 115–118), the whole ending with the so-called "blessing of the song."

Then the disciples began to argue among themselves about who would be the greatest among them. Jesus told them, "In this world the kings and great men lord it over their people, yet they are called 'friends of the people.' But among you it will be different. Those who are the greatest among you should take the lowest rank, and the leader should be like a servant. Who is more important, the one who sits at the table or the one who serves? The one who sits at the table, of course. But not here! For I am among you as one who serves.

"You have stayed with me in my time of trial. And just as my Father has granted me a Kingdom, I now grant you the right to eat and drink at my table in my Kingdom. And you will sit on thrones, judging the twelve tribes of Israel."

Before the Passover celebration, Jesus knew that his hour had come to leave this world and return to his Father. He had loved his disciples during his ministry on earth, and now he loved them to the very end. It was time for supper, and the devil had already prompted Judas, son of Simon Iscariot, to betray Jesus. Jesus knew that the Father had given him authority over everything and that he had come from God and would return to God. So he got up from the table, took off his robe, wrapped a towel around his waist, and poured water into a basin. Then he began to wash the disciples' feet, drying them with the towel he had around him.

When Jesus came to Simon Peter, Peter said to him, "Lord, are you going to wash my feet?"

Jesus replied, "You don't understand now what I am doing, but someday you will."

"No," Peter protested, "you will never ever wash my feet!"

Jesus replied, "Unless I wash you, you won't belong to me."

Simon Peter exclaimed, "Then wash my hands and head as well, Lord, not just my feet!"

Jesus replied, "A person who has bathed all over does not need to wash, except for the feet, to be entirely clean. And you disciples are clean, but not all of you." For Jesus knew who would betray him. That is what he meant when he said, "Not all of you are clean."

After washing their feet, he put on his robe again and sat down and asked, "Do you understand what I was doing? You call me ' Teacher' and 'Lord,' and you are right, because that's what I am. And since I, your Lord and Teacher, have washed your feet, you ought to wash each other's feet. I have given you an example to follow. Do as I have done to you. I tell you the truth, slaves are not greater than their master. Nor is the messenger more important than the one who sends the message. Now that you know these things, God will bless you for doing them.

"I am not saying these things to all of you; I know the ones I have chosen. But this fulfills the Scripture that says, 'The one who eats my food has turned against me.' I tell you this beforehand, so that when it happens you will believe that I AM the Messiah. I tell you the truth, anyone who welcomes my messenger is welcoming me, and anyone who welcomes me is welcoming the Father who sent me."

〇⌒〇

Now, as they were at the table eating, Jesus was deeply troubled, and he exclaimed, "I tell you the truth, one of you eating with me here will betray me!"

The disciples looked at each other, wondering whom he could mean.

Greatly distressed, each one asked in turn, "Am I the one, Lord?"

He replied, "One of you who has just eaten from this bowl with me will betray me. For the Son of Man must die, as the Scriptures declared long ago. But how terrible it will be for the one who betrays him. It would be far better for that man if he had never been born!"

The disciples began to ask each other which of them would ever do such a thing.

Judas, the one who would betray him, also asked, "Rabbi, am I the one?"

And Jesus told him, "You have said it."

The disciple Jesus loved[38] was sitting next to Jesus at the table. Simon Peter motioned to him to ask, "Who's he talking about?" So that disciple leaned over to Jesus and asked, "Lord, who is it?"

Jesus responded, "It is the one to whom I give the bread I dip in the bowl." And when he had dipped it, he gave it to Judas, son of Simon Iscariot. When Judas had eaten the bread, Satan entered into him. Then Jesus told him, "Hurry and do what you're going to do." None of the others at the table

How does Jesus demonstrate being a servant leader to His followers, His disciples?

The disciples continue to be concerned about who is the greatest. Jesus demonstrated love and service because of his relationship with the Father. Which perspective occupies your heart and mind more at this time in your life?

---

[38] **The disciple Jesus loved:** A description that John uses to describe himself in his Gospel.

knew what Jesus meant. Since Judas was their treasurer, some thought Jesus was telling him to go and pay for the food or to give some money to the poor. So Judas left at once, going out into the night.

Then Jesus took a cup of wine and gave thanks to God for it. He said, "Take this and share it among yourselves. For I will not drink wine again until the Kingdom of God has come."

As they were eating, Jesus took some bread and blessed it. Then he broke it in pieces and gave it to the disciples, saying, "Take this and eat it, for this is my body. Do this to remember me."

After supper he took a cup of wine and gave thanks to God for it. He gave it to them and said, "Each of you drink from it, to remember me. For this is my blood, which confirms the new covenant between God and his people. It is poured out as a sacrifice to forgive the sins of many. Mark my words—I will not drink wine again until the day I drink it new with you in my Father's Kingdom." And they all drank from it.[39]

As soon as Judas left the room, Jesus said, "The time has come for the Son of Man to enter into his glory, and God will be glorified because of him. And since God receives glory because of the Son, he will soon give glory to the Son. Dear children, I will be with you only a little longer. And as I told the Jewish leaders, you will search for me, but you can't come where I am going. So now I am giving you a new commandment: Love each other. Just as I have

---

[39] Paul writes to the Corinthian church years later about the meaning of communion. In 1 Corinthians 11:26, Paul says: "For every time you eat this bread and drink this cup, you are announcing the Lord's death until he comes again."

loved you, you should love each other. Your love for one another will prove to the world that you are my disciples."

Simon Peter asked, "Lord, where are you going?"

And Jesus replied, "You can't go with me now, but you will follow me later."

"But why can't I come now, Lord?" he asked. "I'm ready to die for you."

Jesus told them, "Tonight all of you will desert me. For the Scriptures say,

'God will strike the Shepherd, and the sheep of the flock will be scattered.'

But after I have been raised from the dead, I will go ahead of you to Galilee and meet you there."

Peter declared, "Even if everyone else deserts you, I will never desert you."

"Simon, Simon, Satan has asked to sift each of you like wheat. But I have pleaded in prayer for you, Simon, that your faith should not fail. So when you have repented and turned to me again, strengthen your brothers."

Peter said, "Lord, I am ready to go to prison with you, and even to die with you."

Jesus replied, "I tell you the truth, Peter—this very night, before the rooster crows twice, you will deny three times that you even know me."

"No!" Peter declared emphatically. "Even if I have to die with you, I will never deny you!" And all the others vowed the same.

Reflection

What new covenant did Jesus give? What new command did He give?

Look at Peter and the other disciples. What would you have been thinking and feeling if you had been with them that night?

This is Jesus' farewell summary of His life,
ministry and teachings. He wants to drive home
three critical facts: He is leaving; the apostles will
continue Jesus' mission with opposition from the
world; the Holy Spirit will assist them in this
mission. It is a "good news, bad news" scenario.
What lies ahead will be difficult, but Jesus'
promises are out of this world!

Then Jesus asked them, "When I sent you out to preach the Good News and you did not have money, a traveler's bag, or extra clothing, did you need any-thing?"

"No," they replied.

"But now," he said, "take your money and a traveler's bag. And if you don't have a sword, sell your cloak and buy one! For the time has come for this prophecy about me to be fulfilled: 'He was counted among the rebels.' Yes, everything written about me by the prophets will come true."

"Look, Lord," they replied, "we have two swords among us."

"That's enough," he said.

"Don't let your hearts be troubled. Trust in God, and trust also in me. There is more than enough room in my Father's home. If this were not so, would I have told you that I am going to prepare a place for you? When everything is ready, I will come and get you, so that you will always be with me where I am. And you know the way to where I am going."

"No, we don't know, Lord," Thomas said. "We have no idea where you are going, so how can we know the way?"

Jesus told him, "I am the way, the truth, and the life. No one can come to the Father except through me. If you had really known me, you would know who my Father is. From now on, you do know him and have seen him!"

Philip said, "Lord, show us the Father, and we will be satisfied."

Jesus replied, "Have I been with you all this time, Philip, and yet you still don't know who I am? Anyone who has seen me has seen the Father! So why are you asking me to show him to you? Don't you believe that I am in the Father and the Father is in me? The words I speak are not my own, but my Father who lives in me does his work through me. Just believe that I am in the Father and the Father is in me. Or at least believe because of the work you have seen me do.

"I tell you the truth, anyone who believes in me will do the same works I have done, and even greater works, because I am going to be with the Father. You can ask for anything in my name, and I will do it, so that the Son can bring glory to the Father. Yes, ask me for anything in my name, and I will do it!

"If you love me, obey my commandments. And I will ask the Father, and he will give you another Advocate, who will never leave you. He is the Holy Spirit, who leads into all truth. The world cannot receive him, because it isn't looking for him and doesn't recognize him. But you know him, because he lives with you now and later will be in you. No, I will not abandon you as orphans—I will come to you. Soon the world will no longer see me, but you will see me. Since I live, you also will live. When I am raised to life again, you will know that I am in my

Father, and you are in me, and I am in you. Those who accept my commandments and obey them are the ones who love me. And because they love me, my Father will love them. And I will love them and reveal myself to each of them."

Judas (not Judas Iscariot, but the other disciple with that name) said to him, "Lord, why are you going to reveal yourself only to us and not to the world at large?"

Jesus replied, "All who love me will do what I say. My Father will love them, and we will come and make our home with each of them. Anyone who doesn't love me will not obey me. And remember, my words are not my own. What I am telling you is from the Father who sent me. I am telling you these things now while I am still with you. But when the Father sends the Advocate as my representative— that is, the Holy Spirit—he will teach you everything and will remind you of everything I have told you.

"I am leaving you with a gift—peace of mind and heart. And the peace I give is a gift the world cannot give. So don't be troubled or afraid. Remember what I told you: I am going away, but I will come back to you again. If you really loved me, you would be happy that I am going to the Father, who is greater than I am. I have told you these things before they happen so that when they do happen, you will believe.

"I don't have much more time to talk to you, because the ruler of this world approaches. He has no power over me, but I will do what the Father requires of me, so that the world will know that I love the Father. Come, let's be going.

"I am the true grapevine, and my Father is the gardener. He cuts off every branch of mine that doesn't produce fruit, and he prunes the branches that do bear fruit so they will produce even more. You have already been pruned and purified by the message I have given you. Remain in me, and I will remain in you. For a branch cannot produce fruit if it is severed from the vine, and you cannot be fruitful unless you remain in me.

"Yes, I am the vine; you are the branches. Those who remain in me, and I in them, will produce much fruit. For apart from me you can do nothing. Anyone who does not remain in me is thrown away like a useless branch and withers. Such branches are gathered into a pile to be burned. But if you remain in me and my words remain in you, you may ask for anything you want, and it will be granted! When you produce much fruit, you are my true disciples. This brings great glory to my Father.

"I have loved you even as the Father has loved me. Remain in my love. When you obey my command-ments, you remain in my love, just as I obey my Father's commandments and remain in his love. I have told you these things so that you will be filled with my joy. Yes, your joy will overflow! This is my com-mandment: Love each other in the same way I have loved you. There is no greater love than to lay down one's life for one's friends. You are my friends if you do what I command. I no longer call you slaves, because a master doesn't confide in his slaves. Now you are my friends, since I have told you everything the Father told me. You didn't choose me. I chose you. I appointed you to go and produce lasting fruit, so that the Father will give you

Reflection

What did Jesus say is the work of the Holy Spirit?

Which of Jesus' promises to His followers gives you the most comfort? The most challenge?

whatever you ask for, using my name. This is my command: Love each other.

∽

"If the world hates you, remember that it hated me first. The world would love you as one of its own if you belonged to it, but you are no longer part of the world. I chose you to come out of the world, so it hates you. Do you remember what I told you? 'A slave is not greater than the master.' Since they persecuted me, naturally they will persecute you. And if they had listened to me, they would listen to you. They will do all this to you because of me, for they have rejected the One who sent me. They would not be guilty if I had not come and spoken to them. But now they have no excuse for their sin. Anyone who hates me also hates my Father. If I hadn't done such miraculous signs among them that no one else could do, they would not be guilty. But as it is, they have seen everything I did, yet they still hate me and my Father. This fulfills what is written in their Scriptures: 'They hated me without cause.'

"But I will send you the Advocate—the Spirit of truth. He will come to you from the Father and will testify all about me. And you must also testify about me because you have been with me from the beginning of my ministry.

"I have told you these things so that you won't abandon your faith. For you will be expelled from the synagogues, and the time is coming when those who kill you will think they are doing a holy service for God. This is because they have never known the Father or me. Yes, I'm telling you these things now, so that when they happen, you will remember my warning. I didn't tell you earlier because I was going to be with you for a while longer.

"But now I am going away to the One who sent me, and not one of you is asking where I am going. Instead, you grieve because of what I've told you. But in fact, it is best for you that I go away, because if I don't, the Advocate won't come. If I do go away, then I will send him to you. And when he comes, he will convict the world of its sin, and of God's righteousness, and of the coming judgment. The world's sin is that it refuses to believe in me. Righteousness is available because I go to the Father, and you will see me no more. Judgment will come because the ruler of this world has already been judged.

"There is so much more I want to tell you, but you can't bear it now. When the Spirit of truth comes, he will guide you into all truth. He will not speak on his own but will tell you what he has heard. He will tell you about the future. He will bring me glory by telling you whatever he receives from me. All that belongs to the Father is mine; this is why I said, 'The Spirit will tell you whatever he receives from me.'

"In a little while you won't see me anymore. But a little while after that, you will see me again."

Some of the disciples asked each other, "What does he mean when he says, 'In a little while you won't see me, but then you will see me,' and 'I am going to the Father'? And what does he mean by 'a little while'? We don't understand."

Jesus realized they wanted to ask him about it, so he said, "Are you asking yourselves what I meant? I said in a little while you won't see me, but a little while after that you will see me again. I tell you the truth, you will weep and mourn over what is going to happen to me, but the world will rejoice. You will grieve, but your grief will suddenly turn to wonderful joy. It will be like a woman suffering the pains of labor. When her child is born, her anguish gives way to joy because she has brought a new baby into the world. So you have sorrow now, but I will see you again; then you will rejoice, and no one can rob you of that joy. At that time you won't need to ask me for anything. I tell you the truth, you will ask the Father directly, and he will grant your request because you use my name. You haven't done this before. Ask, using my name, and you will receive, and you will have abundant joy.

"I have spoken of these matters in figures of speech, but soon I will stop speaking figuratively and will tell you plainly all about the Father. Then you will ask in my name. I'm not saying I will ask the Father on your behalf, for the Father himself loves you dearly because you love me and believe that I came from God. Yes, I came from the Father into the world, and now I will leave the world and return to the Father."

Then his disciples said, "At last you are speaking plainly and not figuratively. Now we understand that you know everything, and there's no need to question you. From this we believe that you came from God."

Jesus asked, "Do you finally believe? But the time is coming—indeed it's here now—when you will be scattered, each one going his own way, leaving me alone. Yet I am not alone because the Father is with me. I have told you all this so that you may have peace in me. Here on earth you will have many trials and sorrows. But take heart, because I have overcome the world."

Reflection

~~~

After saying all these things, Jesus looked up to heaven and said, "Father, the hour has come. Glorify your Son so he can give glory back to you. For you have given him authority over everyone. He gives eternal life to each one you have given him. And this is the way to have eternal life—to know you, the only true God, and Jesus Christ, the one you sent to earth. I brought glory to you here on earth by completing the work you gave me to do. Now, Father, bring me into the glory we shared before the world began.

"I have revealed you to the ones you gave me from this world. They were always yours. You gave them to me, and they have kept your word. Now they know that everything I have is a gift from you, for I have passed on to them the message you gave me. They accepted it and know that I came from you, and they believe you sent me.

"My prayer is not for the world, but for those you have given me, because they belong to you. All who are mine belong to you, and you have given them to me, so they bring me glory. Now I am departing from the world; they are staying in this world, but I am coming to you. Holy Father, you have given me your name; now protect them by the power of your name so that they will be united just as we are. During my time here, I protected them by the power of the name you gave me. I guarded them so that not one was lost, except the one headed for destruction, as the Scriptures foretold.

Reflection

⚙ What does Jesus warn his followers? What does He promise?

💗 How are you growing in your understanding of the Holy Spirit?

"Now I am coming to you. I told them many things while I was with them in this world so they would be filled with my joy. I have given them your word. And the world hates them because they do not belong to the world, just as I do not belong to the world. I'm not asking you to take them out of the world, but to keep them safe from the evil one. They do not belong to this world any more than I do. Make them holy by your truth; teach them your word, which is truth. Just as you sent me into the world, I am sending them into the world. And I give myself as a holy sacrifice for them so they can be made holy by your truth.

"I am praying not only for these disciples but also for all who will ever believe in me through their message. I pray that they will all be one, just as you and I are one—as you are in me, Father, and I am in you. And may they be in us so that the world will believe you sent me.

"I have given them the glory you gave me, so they may be one as we are one. I am in them and you are in me. May they experience such perfect unity that the world will know that you sent me and that you love them as much as you love me. Father, I want these whom you have given me to be with me where I am. Then they can see all the glory you gave me because you loved me even before the world began!

"O righteous Father, the world doesn't know you, but I do; and these disciples know you sent me. I have revealed you to them, and I will continue to do so. Then your love for me will be in them, and I will be in them."

Then they sang a hymn[40] and went out to the Mount of Olives.

After Jesus prays for the disciples and for us, the real "Lord's Prayer," the band of 11 (remember Judas Iscariot has left them) travels out and around the southern end of the Temple, crossing the Kidron Valley. The blood from the sacrifices in the Temple was directed out of the Temple and down into the Kidron brook flowing into the valley. On that night, with the full moon of the Passover, Jesus would have had to cross the blood and water to make His way to the Mount of Olives for prayer—no doubt reminding Him of His sacrificial blood that would flow soon enough. But before that, He had a destiny that would try His soul!

❧

Scripture References

Matthew 26:17–35; Mark 14:12–31; Luke 22:7–38; John 13–17; 1 Corinthians 11:23–26

Reflection

What does Jesus ask of his Father on behalf of His followers, His disciples?

God has given all believers to Jesus. He prays for them to experience unity in such a way that the world will know that God loves them like He loves Jesus. How are you personally pursuing this unity?

---

[40] One of the Hallel Psalms (Psalms 115–118).

Chapter 12

Jesus' Gethsemane Prayer, Trials and Death

After the Passover, and the incredible teaching of the upper room, Jesus and His now 11 followers leave the room and traverse the southern end of the Temple Mount, going downhill toward the Kidron Valley then up the other side on what was called the Mount of Olives. This area was and still is filled with orchards of olives. The term "Gethsemane" literally translated means "press oil" or olive press. When harvested olives are crushed and pressed, they produce oil that has a multitude of benefits. What a fitting place for our Lord to be "crushed and pressed" by the pressure of our sin, that we might receive abundant benefits.

Then Jesus went with them as usual to the olive grove called Gethsemane, and he said, "Sit here while I go over there to pray. Pray that you will not give in to temptation." He took Peter and Zebedee's two sons, James and John, and he became anguished and distressed. He told them, "My soul is crushed with grief to the point of death. Stay here and keep watch with me."

He went on a little farther, about a stone's throw, and fell with his face to the ground. He prayed that, if it were possible, the awful hour awaiting him might pass him by. "Abba, Father," he cried out, "everything is possible for you. Please take this cup of suffering away from me. Yet I want your will to be done, not mine."

Then an angel from heaven appeared and strengthened him. He prayed more fervently, and he was in such agony of spirit that his sweat fell to the ground like great drops of blood.

At last he stood up again and returned to the disciples and found them asleep, exhausted from grief. "Why are you sleeping?" he asked them. He said to Peter, "Couldn't you watch with me even one hour? Keep watch and pray, so that you will not give in to temptation. For the spirit is willing, but the body is weak!"

Then Jesus left them a second time and prayed, "My Father! If this cup cannot be taken away unless I drink it, your will be done." When he returned to them again, he found them sleeping, for they couldn't keep their eyes open. And they didn't know what to say.

So he went to pray a third time, saying the same things again. Then he came to the disciples and said, "Go ahead and sleep. Have your rest. But look—the time has come. The Son of Man is betrayed into the hands of sinners. Up, let's be going. Look, my betrayer is here!"

Judas, the betrayer, knew this place, because Jesus had often gone there with his disciples. The leading priests, teachers of the religious law, the elders, and Pharisees had given Judas a contingent of Roman soldiers and Temple guards to accompany him. Now with blazing torches, lanterns, and weapons, they arrived at the olive grove.

Jesus fully realized all that was going to happen to him, so he stepped forward to meet them. "Who are you looking for?" he asked.

"Jesus the Nazarene," they replied.

"I AM he," Jesus said. (Judas, who betrayed him, was standing with them.) As Jesus said "I AM he," they all drew back and fell to the ground! Once more he asked them, "Who are you looking for?"

And again they replied, "Jesus the Nazarene."

"I told you that I AM he," Jesus said. "And since I am the one you want, let these others go." He did this to fulfill his own statement: "I did not lose a single one of those you have given me."

The traitor, Judas, had given them a prearranged signal: "You will know which one to arrest when I greet him with a kiss. Then you can take him away under guard." Judas walked up to Jesus. "Greetings, Rabbi!" he exclaimed, and gave him the kiss.

But Jesus said, "Judas, would you betray the Son of Man with a kiss? My friend, go ahead and do what you have come for." Then the others grabbed Jesus and arrested him.

When the other disciples saw what was about to happen, they exclaimed, "Lord, should we fight? We brought the swords!" Then Simon Peter pulled out his sword and struck the high priest's slave, Malchus, slashing off his ear.

"No more of this. Put away your sword," Jesus told him. "Those who use the sword will die by the sword. Shall I not drink from the cup of suffering the Father has given me? Don't you realize that I could ask my Father for thousands of angels to protect us, and he would send them instantly? But if I did, how would the Scriptures be fulfilled that describe what must happen now?" And he touched the man's ear and healed him.

Then Jesus spoke to the leading priests, the captains of the Temple guard, and the elders who had come for him. "Am I some dangerous revolutionary," he asked, "that you come with swords and clubs to arrest me? Why didn't you arrest me in the Temple? I was there among you teaching every day. But this is your moment, the time when the power of darkness reigns. This is all happening to fulfill the words of the prophets as recorded in the Scriptures." At that point, all the disciples deserted him and fled. One young man following behind was clothed only in a long linen shirt. When the mob tried to grab him, he slipped out of his shirt and ran away naked.[41] So the soldiers, their commanding officer, and the Temple guards arrested Jesus and tied him up.

The Jewish government, called the Sanhedrin, was allowed to function independently, but was subject to the Roman occupying force and Empire rule. This group consisted of 70 leaders of the Jewish people from both primary theological groups, the Pharisees and Sadducees. They hated Jesus for different reasons. The Pharisees despised Jesus because He didn't fit into their system of rules and wasn't militant toward the Roman Empire. The Sadducees hated Jesus because He was a threat to their balance of power, and they feared that it could lead to more force exerted by the

Reflection

For what was Jesus praying in the garden of Gethsemane?

When have you found yourself in the condition where your spirit was willing but the body was weak?

---

[41] Most scholars believe this young man was Mark, one of the four Gospel writers. He fits the description, plus this is such a minor detail that only the person it happened to would find it significant enough to include!

Romans. Because of this they had continually tried to defame, arrest, or kill Jesus. Annas had been the high priest but was deposed by the Romans. Cleverly, he arranged for his son-in-law, Caiaphas, to be his successor. But Annas still was the power behind the position! According to Jewish law a capital offense had to be tried on two separate days. Bringing Jesus before Annas late that night and Caiaphas early the next morning was a cunning way to rush Jesus through a trial before most could know what was happening!

First they took him to Annas, the father-in-law of Caiaphas, the high priest at that time. Caiaphas was the one who had told the other Jewish leaders, "It's better that one man should die for the people."

Inside, the high priest began asking Jesus about his followers and what he had been teaching them. Jesus replied, "Everyone knows what I teach. I have preached regularly in the synagogues and the Temple, where the people gather. I have not spoken in secret. Why are you asking me this question? Ask those who heard me. They know what I said."

Then one of the Temple guards standing nearby slapped Jesus across the face. "Is that the way to answer the high priest?" he demanded.

Jesus replied, "If I said anything wrong, you must prove it. But if I'm speaking the truth, why are you beating me?"

Then Annas bound Jesus and sent him to Caiaphas, the high priest.

The leading priests and the entire high council were trying to find evidence against Jesus, so they could put him to death. But they couldn't find any. Many false witnesses spoke against him, but they contradicted each other. Finally, two men stood up and gave this false testimony: "We heard him say, 'I will destroy this Temple made with human hands, and in three days I will build another, made without human hands.'" But even then they didn't get their stories straight!

Then the high priest stood up before the others and asked Jesus, "Well, aren't you going to answer these charges? What do you have to say for yourself?" But Jesus remained silent. The high priest said to him, "I demand in the name of the living God—tell us if you are the Messiah, the Son of God."

Jesus replied, "You have said it. And in the future you will see the Son of Man seated in the place of power at God's right hand and coming on the clouds of heaven."

Then the high priest tore his clothing to show his horror and said, "Blasphemy! Why do we need other witnesses? You have all heard his blasphemy. What is your verdict?"

"Guilty!" they shouted. "He deserves to die!"

Then the guards in charge of Jesus began to spit in his face, and they blindfolded him and beat him with their fists. And some slapped him, jeering, "Prophesy to us, you Messiah! Who hit you that time?" And the guards slapped him as they took him away. And they hurled all sorts of terrible insults at him.

Meanwhile, Simon Peter had followed Jesus at a distance, as did another of the disciples. That other disciple was acquainted with the high priest, so he was allowed to enter the high priest's courtyard with Jesus. Peter had to stay outside the gate. Then the disciple who knew the high priest spoke to the woman watching at the gate, and she let Peter in. One of the servant girls who worked for the high priest came by and noticed Peter warming himself at the fire. She looked at him closely in the firelight and said, "You were one of those with Jesus of Nazareth."

But Peter denied it in front of everyone. "I don't know what you're talking about," he said, and he went out into the entryway. Just then, a rooster crowed.

Later, out by the gate, when another servant girl saw him standing there, she began telling the others, "This man is definitely one of them!"

Again Peter denied it, this time with an oath. "I don't even know the man," he said.

About an hour later some of the other bystanders came over to Peter and insisted, "You must be one of them. We can tell by your Galilean accent."

One of the household slaves of the high priest, a relative of the man whose ear Peter had cut off, asked, "Didn't I see you out there in the olive grove with Jesus?"

Peter swore, "A curse on me if I'm lying—I don't know this man you're talking about!" And immediately the rooster crowed the second time.

At that moment the Lord turned and looked at Peter. Suddenly the Lord's words flashed through Peter's mind: "Before the rooster crows twice, you will deny three times that you even know me." And Peter left the courtyard, broke down, and wept bitterly.

At daybreak all the elders of the people assembled, including the leading priests and the teachers of religious law, to lay plans for putting Jesus to death. Jesus was led before this high council, and they said, "Tell us, are you the Messiah?"

But he replied, "If I tell you, you won't believe me. And if I ask you a question, you won't answer. But from now on the Son of Man will be seated in the place of power at God's right hand." They all shouted, "So, are you claiming to be the Son of God?"

And he replied, "You say that I am."

"Why do we need other witnesses?" they said. "We ourselves heard him say it."

When Judas, who had betrayed him, realized that Jesus had been condemned to die, he was filled with remorse. So he took the thirty pieces of silver back to the leading priests and the elders. "I have sinned," he declared, "for I have betrayed an innocent man."

"What do we care?" they retorted. "That's your problem."

Then Judas threw the silver coins down in the Temple and went out and hanged himself. Falling headfirst there, his body split open, spilling out all his intestines.

The leading priests picked up the coins. "It wouldn't be right to put this money in the Temple treasury," they said, "since it was payment for murder." After some discussion they finally decided to buy the potter's field, and they made it into a cemetery for foreigners. That is why the field is still called the Field of Blood. This fulfilled the prophecy of Jeremiah that says,

Reflection

Describe what Jesus experienced at this point of his trial?

Peter denied Jesus and it only took a look from Jesus to remind him. How does the Holy Spirit remind you of God's words and ways?

"They took the thirty pieces of silver—the price at which he was valued by the people of Israel, and purchased the potter's field, as the LORD directed."

Jesus' trial before Caiaphas ended in the early hours of the morning. Then he was taken to the headquarters of Pilate, the Roman governor. His accusers didn't go inside because it would defile them, and they wouldn't be allowed to celebrate the Passover. So Pilate, the governor, went out to them and asked, "What is your charge against this man?"

"We wouldn't have handed him over to you if he weren't a criminal!" they retorted.

"Then take him away and judge him by your own law," Pilate told them.

"Only the Romans are permitted to execute someone," the Jewish leaders replied. (This fulfilled Jesus' prediction about the way he would die.) They began to state their case: "This man has been leading our people astray by telling them not to pay their taxes to the Roman government and by claiming he is the Messiah, a king."

Then Pilate went back into his headquarters and called for Jesus to be brought to him. "Are you the king of the Jews?" he asked him.

Jesus replied, "Is this your own question, or did others tell you about me?"

"Am I a Jew?" Pilate retorted. "Your own people and their leading priests brought you to me for trial. Why? What have you done?"

Jesus answered, "My Kingdom is not an earthly kingdom. If it were, my followers would fight to keep me from being handed over to the Jewish leaders. But my Kingdom is not of this world."

Pilate said, "So you are a king?"

Jesus responded, "You say I am a king. Actually, I was born and came into the world to testify to the truth. All who love the truth recognize that what I say is true."

"What is truth?" Pilate asked. Then he went out again to the people and told them, "He is not guilty of any crime."

But when the leading priests and the elders made their accusations against him, Jesus remained silent. "Aren't you going to answer them? Don't you hear all these charges they are bringing against you?" Pilate demanded. But Jesus made no response to any of the charges, much to the governor's surprise.

Then the Jewish leaders became insistent. "But he is causing riots by his teaching wherever he goes—all over Judea, from Galilee to Jerusalem!"

The Romans separated the regions of Galilee and Judea into separate provinces for government. Pilate was the Roman governor of Judea and Herod, the governor of Galilee.

"Oh, is he a Galilean?" Pilate asked. When they said that he was, Pilate sent him to Herod Antipas, because Galilee was under Herod's jurisdiction, and Herod happened to be in Jerusalem at the time.

Herod was delighted at the opportunity to see Jesus, because he had heard about him and had been hoping for a long time to see him perform a miracle. He asked Jesus question after question, but Jesus refused to answer. Meanwhile, the leading priests and the teachers of religious law stood there shouting their accusations. Then Herod and his soldiers began mocking and ridiculing Jesus. Finally, they put a royal robe on him and sent him back to Pilate. (Herod and Pilate, who had been enemies before, became friends that day.)

Then Pilate called together the leading priests and other religious leaders, along with the people, and he announced his verdict. "You brought this man to me, accusing him of leading a revolt. I have examined him thoroughly on this point in your presence and find him innocent. Herod came to the same conclusion and sent him back to us. Nothing this man has done calls for the death penalty. So I will have him flogged, and then I will release him."

Now it was the governor's custom each year during the Passover celebration to release one prisoner—anyone the people requested. One of the prisoners at that time was Barabbas, a notorious revolutionary who had committed murder in an uprising. The crowd went to Pilate and asked him to release a prisoner as usual.

"Would you like me to release Barabbas or this 'King of the Jews,' Jesus, who is called Messiah?" Pilate asked. (For he realized by now that the leading priests had arrested Jesus out of envy.)

Just then, as Pilate was sitting on the judgment seat, his wife sent him this message: "Leave that innocent man alone. I suffered through a terrible nightmare about him last night."

Meanwhile, the leading priests and the elders persuaded the crowd to ask for Barabbas to be released and for Jesus to be put to death. So the governor asked again, "Which of these two do you want me to release to you?"

Then a mighty roar rose from the crowd, and with one voice they shouted, "Kill him, and release Barabbas to us!"

Pilate argued with them, because he wanted to release Jesus. "Then what should I do with Jesus who is called the Messiah?"

They kept shouting, "Crucify him! Crucify him!"

For the third time he demanded, "Why? What crime has he committed? I have found no reason to sentence him to death. So I will have him flogged, and then I will release him."

But the mob roared even louder, "Crucify him!"

Some of the governor's soldiers took Jesus into their headquarters and called out the entire regiment.

The soldiers wove a crown of thorns and put it on his head, and they stripped him and put a purple robe on him. Then they knelt before him in mockery and taunted, "Hail! King of the Jews!" And they slapped him across the face.

And they struck him on the head with a reed stick, spit on him, and dropped to their knees in mock worship.

Pilate went outside again and said to the people, "I am going to bring him out to you now, but understand clearly that I find him not guilty." Then Jesus came out wearing the crown of thorns and the purple robe. And Pilate said, "Look, here is the man!"

When they were finally tired of mocking him, they took off the purple robe and put his own clothes on him again.

"Take him yourselves and crucify him," Pilate said. "I find him not guilty."

The Jewish leaders replied, "By our law he ought to die because he called himself the Son of God."

When Pilate heard this, he was more frightened than ever. He took Jesus back into the headquarters again and asked him, "Where are you from?" But Jesus gave no answer. "Why don't you talk to me?" Pilate demanded. "Don't you realize that I have the power to release you or crucify you?"

Then Jesus said, "You would have no power over me at all unless it were given to you from above. So the one who handed me over to you has the greater sin."

Then Pilate tried to release him, but the Jewish leaders shouted, "If you release this man, you are no 'friend of Caesar.' Anyone who declares himself a king is a rebel against Caesar."

The mob shouted louder and louder, demanding that Jesus be crucified, and their voices prevailed.

When they said this, Pilate brought Jesus out to them again. Then Pilate sat down on the judgment seat on the platform that is called the Stone Pavement (in Hebrew, Gabbatha). It was now about noon on the day of preparation for the Passover. And Pilate said to the people, "Look, here is your king!"

"Away with him," they yelled. "Away with him! Crucify him!"

"What? Crucify your king?" Pilate asked.

"We have no king but Caesar," the leading priests shouted back.

Pilate saw that he wasn't getting anywhere and that a riot was developing. So he sent for a bowl of water and washed his hands before the crowd, saying, "I am innocent of this man's blood. The responsibility is yours!"

And all the people yelled back, "We will take responsibility for his death—we and our children!"

So to pacify the crowd, Pilate released Barabbas to them. He ordered Jesus flogged with a lead-tipped whip, then turned him over to the Roman soldiers to be crucified. So Pilate sentenced Jesus to die as they demanded.

Reflection

🐟 When questioned by Pilate and Herod, how did Jesus respond?

💟 What challenges/encourages you as you look at Jesus during His trial?

೮ᔊ

Then they led him away to be crucified. A passerby named Simon, who was from Cyrene, was coming in from the countryside just then, and the soldiers forced him to carry Jesus' cross. (Simon was the father of Alexander and Rufus.)

A large crowd trailed behind, including many grief-stricken women. But Jesus turned and said to them, "Daughters of Jerusalem, don't weep for me, but weep for yourselves and for your children. For the days are coming when they will say, 'Fortunate indeed are the women who are childless, the wombs that have not borne a child and the breasts that have never nursed.' People will beg the mountains, 'Fall on us,' and plead with the hills, 'Bury us.' For if these things are done when the tree is green, what will happen when it is dry?"

Two others, both criminals, were led out to be executed with him.

And they went out to a place called Golgotha (which means "Place of the Skull" in Hebrew). The soldiers gave him wine mixed with bitter gall, but when he had tasted it, he refused to drink it.

There they nailed him to the cross. Two revolutionaries were crucified with him, one on either side, with Jesus between them.

It was nine o'clock in the morning when they crucified him.

Jesus said, "Father, forgive them, for they don't know what they are doing."

And Pilate posted a sign over him that read, "Jesus of Nazareth, the King of the Jews." The place where Jesus was crucified was near the city, and the sign was written in Hebrew, Latin, and Greek, so that many people could read it.

Then the leading priests objected and said to Pilate, "Change it from 'The King of the Jews' to 'He said, I am King of the Jews.'"

Pilate replied, "No, what I have written, I have written."

When the soldiers had crucified Jesus, they divided his clothes among the four of them. They also took his robe, but it was seamless, woven in one piece from top to bottom. So they said, "Rather than tearing it apart, let's throw dice for it. This fulfilled the Scripture that says, "They divided my garments among themselves and threw dice for my clothing."

So that is what they did. Then they sat around and kept guard as he hung there.

The people passing by shouted abuse, shaking their heads in mockery. "Look at you now!" they yelled at him. "You said you were going to destroy the Temple and rebuild it in three days. Well then, if you are the Son of God, save yourself and come down from the cross!"

The leading priests, the teachers of religious law, and the elders also mocked Jesus. "He saved others," they scoffed, "but he can't save himself! So he is the King of Israel, is he? Let him come down from the cross right now, and we will believe in him! He trusted God, so let God rescue him now if he wants him! For he said, 'I am the Son of God.'"

The soldiers mocked him, too, by offering him a drink of sour wine. They called out to him, "If you are the King of the Jews, save yourself!"

One of the criminals hanging beside him scoffed, "So you're the Messiah, are you? Prove it by saving yourself—and us, too, while you're at it!"

But the other criminal protested, "Don't you fear God even when you have been sentenced to die? We deserve to die for our crimes, but this man hasn't done anything wrong." Then he said, "Jesus, remember me when you come into your Kingdom."

And Jesus replied, "I assure you, today you will be with me in paradise."

Standing near the cross were Jesus' mother, and his mother's sister, Mary (the wife of Clopas), and Mary Magdalene. When Jesus saw his mother standing there beside the disciple he loved, he said to her, "Dear woman, here is your son." And he said to this disciple, "Here is your mother." And from then on this disciple took her into his home.

Reflection

(icon) What stands out to you about the crucifixion of Jesus?

(icon) Jesus was able to forgive even while hanging on the cross. To whom do you need to extend forgiveness?

At noon, darkness fell across the whole land until three o'clock. Then at three o'clock Jesus called out with a loud voice, *"Eli, Eli, lema sabachthani?"* which means "My God, my God, why have you abandoned me?"

Some of the bystanders misunderstood and thought he was calling for the prophet Elijah. Jesus knew that his mission was now finished, and to fulfill Scripture he said, "I am thirsty." A jar of sour wine was sitting there, so they soaked a sponge in it, put it on a hyssop branch, and held it up to his lips.

But the rest said, "Wait! Let's see whether Elijah comes to save him."

When Jesus had tasted it, he said, "It is finished!" Then Jesus shouted, "Father, I entrust my spirit into your hands!" Then he bowed his head and released his spirit.

In the Temple there was a large and elaborate curtain that separated the Holy Place, where numerous priests performed their duties, from the Most Holy Place, which the high priest alone entered annually on the Day of Atonement. When the high priest entered the Most Holy Place, he sprinkled the blood of the sacrificial lamb onto the Ark of the Covenant, which represented God's throne. The entire act symbolized the removal of Israel's sins for the past year. This curtain was 30 feet tall and wide and reportedly extremely thick. It represented the separation of God from man, bridged only by a high priest. What happens next is God's way of

*demonstrating who Jesus is and just what He has
accomplished by His death!*

At that moment the curtain in the sanctuary of
the Temple was torn in two, from top to bottom.
The earth shook, rocks split apart, and tombs
opened. The bodies of many godly men and women
who had died were raised from the dead. They left
the cemetery after Jesus' resurrection, went into the
holy city of Jerusalem, and appeared to many people.

The Roman officer and the other soldiers at the
crucifixion were terrified by the earthquake and all
that had happened. When the Roman officer who
stood facing Jesus saw how he had died, he
exclaimed, "This man truly was the Son of God!"
And when all the crowd that came to see the
crucifixion saw what had happened, they went home
in deep sorrow.

Many women who had come from Galilee with
Jesus to care for him were watching from a distance.
Among them were Mary Magdalene, Mary (the
mother of James and Joseph), and Salome, the
mother of James and John, the sons of Zebedee.

It was the day of preparation, and the Jewish
leaders didn't want the bodies hanging there the next
day, which was the Sabbath (and a very special
Sabbath, because it was the Passover). So they asked
Pilate to hasten their deaths by ordering that their
legs be broken. Then their bodies could be taken
down. So the soldiers came and broke the legs of the
two men crucified with Jesus. But when they came
to Jesus, they saw that he was already dead, so they
didn't break his legs. One of the soldiers, however,
pierced his side with a spear, and immediately blood
and water flowed out. (This report is from an

eyewitness giving an accurate account. He speaks the truth so that you also can believe.) These things happened in fulfillment of the Scriptures that say, "Not one of his bones will be broken," and "They will look on the one they pierced."

Now there was a good and righteous man named Joseph, who had been a secret disciple of Jesus (because he feared the Jewish leaders). He was a member of the Jewish high council, but he had not agreed with the decision and actions of the other religious leaders. He was from the town of Arimathea in Judea, and he was waiting for the Kingdom of God to come. As evening approached, Joseph of Arimathea took a risk and went to Pilate and asked for Jesus' body. Pilate couldn't believe that Jesus was already dead, so he called for the Roman officer and asked if he had died yet. The officer confirmed that Jesus was dead.

When Pilate gave permission, Joseph came and took the body away. With him came Nicodemus, the man who had come to Jesus at night. He brought seventy-five pounds of perfumed ointment made from myrrh and aloes. Following Jewish burial custom, they wrapped Jesus' body with the spices in long sheets of linen cloth. The place of crucifixion was near a garden, where there was a new tomb, never used before. And so, because it was the day of preparation for the Jewish Passover and since the tomb was close at hand, they laid Jesus there. Then Joseph rolled a stone in front of the entrance.

Both Mary Magdalene and the other Mary, the mother of Joseph,[42] were sitting across from the

---

[42] **Joseph:** This is not the same Joseph who took Jesus' body away, but is the brother of James.

tomb and saw where Jesus' body was laid. Then they went home and prepared spices and ointments to anoint his body. But by the time they were finished the Sabbath had begun, so they rested as required by the law.

The next day, on the Sabbath, the leading priests and Pharisees went to see Pilate. They told him, "Sir, we remember what that deceiver once said while he was still alive: 'After three days I will rise from the dead.' So we request that you seal the tomb[43] until the third day. This will prevent his disciples from coming and stealing his body and then telling everyone he was raised from the dead! If that happens, we'll be worse off than we were at first."

Pilate replied, "Take guards and secure it the best you can." So they sealed the tomb and posted guards to protect it.

What incredible emotions took place as a result of these events! For the enemies of Jesus, this day of reckoning had been long in coming. "Good riddance," expressed their sentiments. With Jesus finally out of the way things would settle down, and their power would remain intact. However, for Jesus' followers, when the stone was rolled in front of the tomb, their hope also died! "Heartbroken and hopeless," would describe their emotions. But, as the famous sermon says, "That was Friday . . . Sunday's coming!"

---

[43] Tombs in that region and era were burial chambers. Usually they contained a resting place or two for the recently departed and a small "weeping chamber" for mourners. After the body had decomposed, the skeletal bones were gathered into a box called a sarcophagous and retained.

Reflection

What is the significance of the curtain being torn in two?

Due to fear, Joseph from Aramathia had secretly followed Jesus. He found the courage to ask for Jesus' body. When have you set aside fear and found courage to take the next step in following Jesus?

Scripture References

Matthew 26:36—27:66; Mark 14:32—15:47; Luke 22:39—23:56; John 18:1—19:38; Acts 1:18–19

Timeline of the Day Jesus Died

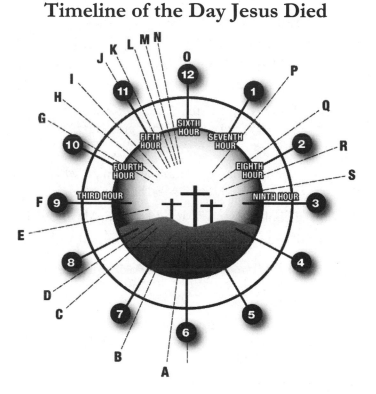

Events Preceding Roman Trial and Crucifixion

    The Last Supper Lk 22:14

    Prayer in Gethsemane Mt 26:36

    Arrest in the Gethsemane Jn 18:12

    Trial at the house of Caiaphas Lk 22:54

The Crucifixion

    A. Before Pilate Mt 27:11

    B. Sent to Herod Lk 23:6–10

    C. Returned to Pilate Lk 23:11

D. Sentenced Lk 23:23–24

E. Led to Calvary Lk 23:26

F. Crucified Lk 23:33

G. Soldiers divided His clothes and cast lots for them Mt 27:35

"Jesus said, 'Father, forgive them, for they don't know what they are doing." Lk 23:34

"It was nine o'clock in the morning when they crucified him." Mk 15:25

H. People passing by insulted Him. Mt 27:39–40

I. The Jewish leaders mocked Him. Mk 15:31

J. The soldiers mocked Him. Lk 23:36–37

K. One of the criminals on the cross mocked Him. Lk 23:39

L. The other criminal on the cross rebukes the man and asks Jesus to remember Him in heaven. Lk 23:40, 42

M. Jesus promises that the criminal will be in heaven with Him that very day. Lk 23:43

N. Jesus tells His mother to care for John and tells John to care for His mother. Jn 19:26–27

O. Darkness covers the land. Mk 15:33

P. Jesus cries out to His Father, asking why He has forsaken His Son. Mt 27:46

Q. Jesus is thirsty. Jn 19:28

R. Jesus says, "It is finished!" Jn 19:30

S. "Father, I entrust my spirit into your hands!" And with these words he breathed his last. Lk 23:46

Events Immediately Following the Crucifixion

The earthquake and tearing in two of the curtain Mt 27:51

Tombs break open Mt 27:52

Roman centurion confesses that Jesus is God's Son Mt 27:54

The sorrow of the multitude Lk 23:48

The criminals' legs are broken. Jn 19:31–32

The soldier pierces Jesus' side. Jn 19:34

The burial Jn 19:38–42

The tomb is secured by a seal and a guard is posted to protect it. Mt 27:66

Chapter 13

Jesus Is ALIVE!

The Hebrew accounting for time was from sundown to sundown. That is why there was such a hurry to remove Jesus' body from the cross and move Him into the tomb. His body was hastily washed and wrapped, with the plan to complete the burial process after Passover, on Sunday, the first day of the week. Those days and nights must have been painful for His followers. Their hearts were broken. When Jesus was killed and buried, their hopes died and were buried with Him. But not only was a new day dawning, a whole new era was beginning! It would be better, more challenging and rewarding than they had ever dreamed!

Saturday evening, when the Sabbath ended, Mary Magdalene and Salome and Mary the mother of James went out and purchased burial spices so they could anoint Jesus' body.

Early on Sunday morning, as the new day was dawning, Mary Magdalene and the other Mary went out to visit the tomb. On the way they were asking each other, "Who will roll away the stone for us from the entrance to the tomb?" Suddenly, as they arrived, there was a great earthquake! For an angel of the Lord came down from heaven, rolled aside the stone, which was very large, and sat on it. His face shone like lightning, and his clothing was as white as snow. The guards shook with fear when they saw him, and they fell into a dead faint.

So they went in, but they didn't find the body of the Lord Jesus. As they stood there puzzled, two men suddenly appeared to them, clothed in dazzling robes.

The women were terrified and bowed with their faces to the ground. Then the men asked, "Why are you looking among the dead for someone who is alive? He isn't here! He is risen from the dead! Remember what he told you back in Galilee, that the Son of Man must be betrayed into the hands of sinful men and be crucified, and that he would rise again on the third day." Then they remembered that he had said this.

"And now, go quickly and tell his disciples, including Peter, that he has risen from the dead, and he is going ahead of you to Galilee. You will see him there, just as he told you before he died. Remember what I have told you."

The women fled from the tomb, trembling and bewildered, and they said nothing to anyone because they were too frightened. So they rushed back from the tomb to tell his eleven disciples—and everyone else—what had happened. It was Mary Magdalene, Joanna, Mary the mother of James, and several other women who told the apostles what had happened. But the story sounded like nonsense to the men, so they didn't believe it.

Reflection

What was the reaction of both the guards and the women upon seeing the angel at the tomb?

What helps you believe in Jesus' resurrection? What may bring doubts?

However, Peter and the other disciple started out for the tomb. They were both running, but the other disciple outran Peter and reached the tomb first. He stooped and looked in and saw the linen wrappings lying there, but he didn't go in. Then

Simon Peter arrived and went inside. He also noticed the linen empty wrappings lying there, while the cloth that had covered Jesus' head was folded up and lying apart from the other wrappings. Then the disciple who had reached the tomb first also went in, and he saw and believed—for until then they still hadn't understood the Scriptures that said Jesus must rise from the dead. Then they went home.

After Jesus rose from the dead early on Sunday morning, the first person who saw him was Mary Magdalene, the woman from whom he had cast out seven demons.

Mary was standing outside the tomb crying, and as she wept, she stooped and looked in. She saw two white-robed angels, one sitting at the head and the other at the foot of the place where the body of Jesus had been lying. "Dear woman, why are you crying?" the angels asked her.

"Because they have taken away my Lord," she replied, "and I don't know where they have put him."

She turned to leave and saw someone standing there. It was Jesus, but she didn't recognize him. "Dear woman, why are you crying?" Jesus asked her. "Who are you looking for?"

She thought he was the gardener. "Sir," she said, "if you have taken him away, tell me where you have put him, and I will go and get him."

"Mary!" Jesus said.

She turned to him and cried out, "Rabboni!" (which is Hebrew for "Teacher").

"Don't cling to me," Jesus said, "for I haven't yet ascended to the Father. But go find my brothers and tell them that I am ascending to my Father and your Father, to my God and your God." Mary Magdalene found the disciples and told them, "I have seen the Lord!" Then she gave them his message. But when she told them that Jesus was alive and she had seen him, they didn't believe her.

The Roman soldiers at Jesus' tomb were dispatched as requested by the Jewish leadership from Pilate, the Roman governor. They were to protect the body from being stolen by Christ's followers. The penalty for failing in their duty was death. So rather than report to their Roman military superiors, they ran to the Jewish authorities for direction and protection.

As the women were on their way, some of the guards went into the city and told the leading priests what had happened. A meeting with the elders was called, and they decided to give the soldiers a large bribe. They told the soldiers, "You must say, 'Jesus' disciples came during the night while we were sleeping, and they stole his body.' If the governor hears about it, we'll stand up for you so you won't get in trouble." So the guards accepted the bribe and said what they were told to say. Their story spread widely among the Jews, and they still tell it today.

Having been devastated by Jesus' death, His many followers began the long journey back to their homes. Although they heard that His body was gone through the initial reports of the women, it was beyond their reason that He could have been resurrected. However, their lives were about to be changed!

Reflection

How did Mary, Peter and the other disciple each react to these events?

Jesus revealed Himself to Mary yet no one believed her. When you've shared your faith, have you experienced the disbelief of others?

That same day two of Jesus' followers were walking to the village of Emmaus, seven miles from Jerusalem. As they walked along they were talking about everything that had happened. As they talked and discussed these things, Jesus himself appeared in a different form and suddenly came and began walking with them. But God kept them from recognizing him.

He asked them, "What are you discussing so intently as you walk along?"

They stopped short, sadness written across their faces. Then one of them, Cleopas, replied, "You must be the only person in Jerusalem who hasn't heard about all the things that have happened there the last few days."

"What things?" Jesus asked.

"The things that happened to Jesus, the man from Nazareth," they said. "He was a prophet who did powerful miracles, and he was a mighty teacher in the eyes of God and all the people. But our leading priests and other religious leaders handed him over to be condemned to death, and they crucified him. We had hoped he was the Messiah who had come to rescue Israel. This all happened three days ago.

"Then some women from our group of his followers were at his tomb early this morning, and they came back with an amazing report. They said his body was missing, and they had seen angels who told them Jesus is alive! Some of our men ran out to see, and sure enough, his body was gone, just as the women had said."

Then Jesus said to them, "You foolish people! You find it so hard to believe all that the prophets wrote in the Scriptures. Wasn't it clearly predicted that the Messiah would have to suffer all these things before entering his glory?" Then Jesus took them through the writings of Moses and all the prophets, explaining from all the Scriptures the things concerning himself.

By this time they were nearing Emmaus and the end of their journey. Jesus acted as if he were going on, but they begged him, "Stay the night with us, since it is getting late." So he went home with them. As they sat down to eat, he took the bread and blessed it. Then he broke it and gave it to them. Suddenly, their eyes were opened, and they recognized him. And at that moment he disappeared!

They said to each other, "Didn't our hearts burn within us as he talked with us on the road and explained the Scriptures to us?" And within the hour they were on their way back to Jerusalem. There they found the eleven disciples and the others who had gathered with them, who said, "The Lord has really risen! He appeared to Peter." That Sunday evening the disciples were meeting behind locked doors because they were afraid of the Jewish leaders.

Reflection

How did Jesus reveal himself to the tow followers heading to Emmaus?

The resurrection was a life changing event in the disciples and followers lives. How has your belief in the resurrected Lord been life changing for you recently?

Then the two from Emmaus told their story of how Jesus had appeared to them as they were walking along the road, and how they had recognized him as he was breaking the bread. And just as they were telling about it, Jesus himself was suddenly standing there among them. "Peace be with you," he said. But the whole group was startled

and frightened, thinking they were seeing a ghost!
He rebuked them for their stubborn unbelief
because they refused to believe those who had seen
him after he had been raised from the dead. "Why
are you frightened?" he asked. "Why are your hearts
filled with doubt? Look at my hands. Look at my
feet. You can see that it's really me. Touch me and
make sure that I am not a ghost, because ghosts
don't have bodies, as you see that I do." As he
spoke, he showed them his hands and his feet.

Still they stood there in disbelief, filled with joy
and wonder. Then he asked them, "Do you have
anything here to eat?" They gave him a piece of
broiled fish, and he ate it as they watched.

As he spoke, he showed them the wounds in
his hands and his side. They were filled with joy
when they saw the Lord! Again he said, "Peace be
with you. As the Father has sent me, so I am
sending you." Then he breathed on them and said,
"Receive the Holy Spirit. If you forgive anyone's
sins, they are forgiven. If you do not forgive them,
they are not forgiven."

One of the twelve disciples, Thomas
(nicknamed the Twin), was not with the others when
Jesus came. They told him, "We have seen the
Lord!"

But he replied, "I won't believe it unless I see
the nail wounds in his hands, put my fingers into
them, and place my hand into the wound in his
side."

Eight days later the disciples were together
again, and this time Thomas was with them. The

Reflection

When the
disciples' eyes
were opened
what did Jesus
give them?

How do
you feel about
as a follower
of Jesus being
given the Holy
Spirit?

doors were locked; but suddenly, as before, Jesus was standing among them. "Peace be with you," he said. Then he said to Thomas, "Put your finger here, and look at my hands. Put your hand into the wound in my side. Don't be faithless any longer. Believe!"

"My Lord and my God!" Thomas exclaimed.

Then Jesus told him, "You believe because you have seen me. Blessed are those who believe without seeing me."

The disciples saw Jesus do many other miraculous signs in addition to the ones recorded in this book. But these are written so that you may continue to believe that Jesus is the Messiah, the Son of God, and that by believing in him you will have life by the power of his name.

Reflection

Overwhelmed and overjoyed, the followers of Christ knew that things had changed forever. Jesus had a plan that He was about to reveal that would not only change their lives but ours—and the whole world—FOREVER! So, the risen Lord instructed the women to tell the apostles to travel to the region of Galilee to meet with Him.

What does Jesus say and do with Thomas?

When you doubt or are fearful how do you respond?

Scripture References

Matthew 28:1–15; Mark 16:1–14; Luke 24:1–43; John 20:1–31

Chapter 14

Jesus' Appearances, Commission and Ascension

Jesus is resurrected! He was dead, and now He is alive! Incredible . . . amazing! But even this isn't the end. It is a new beginning! Not only does He continue to give evidence of His new life and courage to His followers, but He also introduces them to marching orders of their own that will change the world!

Jesus told His followers to meet Him in Galilee, and they did. Waiting for Jesus' next appearance and instructions, Peter, a fisherman by trade, simply does what is natural. But, it turns into a life-changing supernatural experience!

Later, Jesus appeared again to the disciples beside the Sea of Galilee. This is how it happened. Several of the disciples were there—Simon Peter, Thomas (nick-named the Twin), Nathanael from Cana in Galilee, the sons of Zebedee, and two other disciples.

Simon Peter said, "I'm going fishing."

"We'll come, too," they all said. So they went out in the boat, but they caught nothing all night.

At dawn Jesus was standing on the beach, but the disciples couldn't see who he was. He called out, "Fellows, have you caught any fish?"

"No," they replied.

Then he said, "Throw out your net on the right-hand side of the boat, and you'll get some!" So they did, and they couldn't haul in the net because there were so many fish in it.

Then the disciple Jesus loved said to Peter, "It's the Lord!" When Simon Peter heard that it was the Lord, he put on his tunic (for he had stripped for work), jumped into the water, and headed to shore. The others stayed with the boat and pulled the loaded net to the shore, for they were only about a hundred yards from shore. When they got there, they found breakfast waiting for them—fish cooking over a charcoal fire, and some bread.

"Bring some of the fish you've just caught," Jesus said. So Simon Peter went aboard and dragged the net to the shore. There were 153 large fish, and yet the net hadn't torn.

"Now come and have some breakfast!" Jesus said. None of the disciples dared to ask him, "Who are you?" They knew it was the Lord. Then Jesus served them the bread and the fish. This was the third time Jesus had appeared to his disciples since he had been raised from the dead.

> *Familiar? You bet. The coincidences are inevitable. No fish . . . throw nets on other side . . . miraculous catch of fishes . . . the sharing of bread and fish! Jesus is trying to draw them in and remind them of who He is, how He has always loved them and taken care of them, and what He can do. He is preparing them for the next venture of faith that He has prepared for them.*

After breakfast Jesus asked Simon Peter, "Simon son of John, do you love me more than these?"

"Yes, Lord," Peter replied, "you know I love you."

"Then feed my lambs," Jesus told him.

Jesus repeated the question: "Simon son of John, do you love me?" "Yes, Lord," Peter said, "you know I love you."

"Then take care of my sheep," Jesus said.

A third time he asked him, "Simon son of John, do you love me?"

Peter was hurt that Jesus asked the question a third time. He said, "Lord, you know everything. You know that I love you."

Jesus said, "Then feed my sheep.

"I tell you the truth, when you were young, you were able to do as you liked; you dressed yourself and went wherever you wanted to go. But when you are old, you will stretch out your hands, and others will dress you and take you where you don't want to go." Jesus said this to let him know by what kind of death he would glorify God. Then Jesus told him, "Follow me."

Peter turned around and saw behind them the disciple Jesus loved—the one who had leaned over to Jesus during supper and asked, "Lord, who will betray you?" Peter asked Jesus, "What about him, Lord?"

Jesus replied, "If I want him to remain alive until I return, what is that to you? As for you, follow me." So the rumor spread among the community of believers that this disciple wouldn't die. But that isn't what Jesus said at all. He only said, "If I want him to remain alive until I return, what is that to you?"

Then the eleven disciples left for Galilee, going to the mountain where Jesus had told them to go. When they saw him, they worshiped him—but some of them doubted!

Jesus appears and reappears to His followers several times. Even though the disciples ate with Jesus, touched Him, walked with Him and talked with Him, doubt would still linger. This shows the Gospel writer's honesty. The evidence is clear, but it still seems impossible. However, the disciples pressed through this doubt. Jesus never chastised them for it; rather He just gave them more evidence to believe, thus strengthening their resolve.

Jesus came and told his disciples, "I have been given all authority in heaven and on earth. Therefore, go and make disciples of all the nations, baptizing them in the name of the Father and the Son and the Holy Spirit. Teach these new disciples to obey all the commands I have given you. And be sure of this: I am with you always, even to the end of the age.

"Anyone who believes and is baptized will be saved. But anyone who refuses to believe will be condemned. These miraculous signs will accompany those who believe: They will cast out demons in my name, and they will speak in new languages. They will be able to handle snakes with safety, and if they drink anything poisonous, it won't hurt them. They will be able to place their hands on the sick, and they will be healed."

Reflection

What does Jesus do for the disciples? Does this remind you of anything?

If you took a walk with Jesus like Peter what would you discuss? Spend some time in quiet with Jesus today?

Reflection

What does Jesus ask his followers to do?

How do you recognize Jesus' authority and presence in your life? How are you responding to what he said?

After that, he was seen by more than 500 of his followers at one time, most of whom are still alive, though some have died. Then he was seen by James and later by all the apostles.[44]

Then he said, "When I was with you before, I told you that everything written about me in the law of Moses and the prophets and in the Psalms must be fulfilled." Then he opened their minds to understand the Scriptures. And he said, "Yes, it was written long ago that the Messiah would suffer and die and rise from the dead on the third day. It was also written that this message would be proclaimed in the authority of his name to all the nations, beginning in Jerusalem: 'There is forgiveness of sins for all who repent.' You are witnesses of all these things.

"And now I will send the Holy Spirit, just as my Father promised. But stay here in the city until the Holy Spirit comes and fills you with power from heaven."

So the disciples traveled back to Jerusalem as directed. Jesus meets with them again, teaching them, instilling in them His plan for them to take this message of hope, healing and salvation to the whole world! He reassures them that He will be with them and will empower them to accomplish this mission.

During the forty days after his crucifixion, he appeared to the apostles from time to time, and he

Reflection

Jesus said he would send the Holy Spirit. What will the Holy Spirit do?

How have the Scriptures come alive since you have come to know Jesus? Or even since reading through this book?

---

[44] This is an insertion from Paul's writing in 1 Corinthians 15:6–7.

proved to them in many ways that he was actually alive. And he talked to them about the Kingdom of God.

Once when he was eating with them, he commanded them, "Do not leave Jerusalem until the Father sends you the gift he promised, as I told you before. John baptized with water, but in just a few days you will be baptized with the Holy Spirit."

So when the apostles were with Jesus, they kept asking him, "Lord, has the time come for you to free Israel and restore our kingdom?"

He replied, "The Father alone has the authority to set those dates and times, and they are not for you to know. But you will receive power when the Holy Spirit comes upon you. And you will be my witnesses, telling people about me everywhere—in Jerusalem, through-out Judea, in Samaria, and to the ends of the earth."

Then Jesus led them to Bethany,[45] and lifting his hands to heaven, he blessed them. While he was blessing them, he left them and was taken up to heaven while they were watching and they could no longer see him and sat down in the place of honor at God's right hand.

As they strained to see him rising into heaven, two white-robed men suddenly stood among them. "Men of Galilee," they said, "why are you standing here staring into heaven? Jesus has been taken from you into heaven, but someday he will return from heaven in the same way you saw him go!"

---

[45] **Bethany:** Bethany is the town that Lazarus was from and where he was raised from the dead. It is on the upper part of the Mount of Olives across the Kidron Valley and up the slope from the Garden of Gethsemane.

Then the apostles returned to Jerusalem from the Mount of Olives, a distance of half a mile. And they spent all of their time in the Temple, praising God. And the disciples went everywhere and preached, and the Lord worked through them, confirming what they said by many miraculous signs.

***

The disciples saw Jesus do many other miraculous signs in addition to the ones recorded in this book. But these are written so that you may continue to believe that Jesus is the Messiah, the Son of God, and that by believing in him you will have life by the power of his name.

This disciple is the one who testifies to these events and has recorded them here. And we know that his account of these things is accurate.

Jesus also did many other things. If they were all written down, I suppose the whole world could not contain the books that would be written.

Jesus' earthly work is finished. He has accomplished what He has come to do, and it is time to go home. Now He has to get busy with His new work of interceding for the saints at the right hand of the Father. And just as He has promised, He is also preparing a place for us. Finally and perhaps most importantly, the Holy Spirit will come, but only after Jesus' ascension into heaven. Jesus was the only One who could do His job. But now it is up to Jesus to pass the baton to the Holy Spirit. It is the ascension of Jesus that promises His return and thus empowers us to live for eternity in the present absence of our Lord.

Thus, the story of Jesus ends and the annals of His bride, the church, begin. May His power continue to pervade our preaching and our lives until His glorious appearing in the clouds. Come, Lord Jesus!

Scripture References

John 20:26—21:25; 1 Corinthians 15:6–7; Matthew 28:16–20; Mark 16:15–20; Luke 24:44–53; Acts 1:3–12

Reflection

What does Jesus say is next in following Him?

How has your life been impacted by the things written here? What do you believe about Jesus and following Him?

Epilogue

HIS Story has come to an end, or rather, to a beginning. It doesn't end here.

Jesus' followers took His message of redemption and salvation based on His death and resurrection to their known world. In fact, in just one generation they were accused of "turning the world upside down"! It was presented to everyone from slave to free, men to women, rich to poor, commoner to civic leaders, and Jewish to non-Jewish. And that message for over 2,000 years has continued to impact, transform and reach around the world.

HIS Story is really simple. In fulfillment of God's plan, promise and prophecy, He—Jesus came to earth. He lived a life without sin of any sort. In fact, no one—friend, family or enemy—ever accused Him of anything but a spotless life. He taught like no other had ever taught. In fact, His friends and adversaries remarked at His masterful teaching, and the modern world heralds His "Sermon on the Mount" as a masterpiece of moral instruction.   He performed miracles—healing, feeding over 5,000 at one time, walking on water, calming the sea, and more! His most bitter enemies admitted to these miraculous demonstrations of His authority over nature. Above all, He raised the dead back to life . . . not just once, not twice, but three different times! And once again, not only did His followers witness the events, but so did His opposition, without ever denying these miracles.

Ultimately, He said He would go to Jerusalem, be arrested, tried, executed, buried and resurrected.

Yes, He would be alive after three days in the grave. Once again, He didn't say it just once, but over a dozen times! His enemies had no explanation. They even paid soldiers to lie about the resurrection, but they still couldn't produce the body. The evidence for the resurrection is overwhelming!

Dr. John Warwick Montgomery, past Dean of the Simon Greenleaf School of Law, stated,

> "It passes the bounds of credibility that the early Christians could have manufactured such a tale as the empty tomb and then preached it among those who might easily have refuted it by simply **producing the body of Jesus!** It is unreasonable that one historian, one eyewitness, one antagonist would not record for all time that he had seen Christ's [dead] body. The silence of history is deafening when it comes to testimony against the resurrection!"
> [*History and Christianity*]

And now, HIS Story has found its way into your heart and mind. Please don't doubt it. Please don't walk away unchanged. C. S. Lewis said that either Jesus was a Liar, who has convinced the world that He is something that He isn't . . . or a Lunatic with a "messiah" complex who somehow was able to draw and keep an amazing following . . . or He is exactly who He said He is: The Lord!

So what will you do with HIS Story?

If you still doubt or have questions, we beg you to continue seeking the answers!

If you just close HIS Story as another book, we beg you to reconsider its truth and the consequences of denying and rejecting Jesus.

But if you choose to embrace the Man, Message and Miracle that is JESUS, let it sink in . . . let it challenge and change your life . . . let it make you more and more, in every way and every day like Him!

This is why John writes to us:

"The disciples saw Jesus do many other miraculous signs in addition to the ones recorded in this book. But these are written so that you may continue to believe that Jesus is the Messiah, the Son of God, and that by believing in him you will have life by the power of his name." John 20:30–31